SPECIAL DIET COOKBO

BEAT OSTEOPOROSIS

CW00362630

SPECIAL DIET COOKBOOKS

BEAT OSTEOPOROSIS

Delicious calcium-rich recipes to help make stronger bones

Victor G. Ettinger, M. D. with Judy Fredal, R. D.

THORSONS PUBLISHING GROUP

First published 1988 by Perigree Books, The
Putnam Publishing Group, New York 1988
This revised UK edition 1990

British Library Cataloguing in Publication Data

Ettinger, Victor G.
    Beat osteoporosis: delicious calcium-rich
    recipes to help make stronger bones. – Rev.
    UK ed.
    1. Food. High calcium dishes
    I. Title II. Fredal, Judy III. Series
    641. 5632

ISBN 0 7225 2214 2

*Published by Thorsons Publishers Limited,
Wellingborough, Northamptonshire, NN8 2RQ
England*

Printed in Great Britain by The Bath Press, Bath

10 9 8 7 6 5 4 3 2 1

CONTENTS

ACKNOWLEDGEMENTS

Many people, both professional and lay, contributed to the factual content of this book. To list them individually would court the disaster of forgetting one, so we will just thank them en masse: *Thank you*.

In addition, I specifically want to thank Adrienne Ingrum and Anton Mueller from The Putnam Publishing Group, whose attention to the important details made this book happen; and Anna Jardine, whose copyediting makes the words flow like music. Finally I wish to adjoin the mandatory thanks to my family for putting up with my seclusions for long hours in my study while I wrote and revised this manuscript.

And with sincere thanks and appreciation to Theresa and Francis Fredal, Charlene Muranaka, Nancy Ingram, Maria Cardinale and Patty Hall for help in recipe development and testing; Jennifer Mack, Chris Kimball, Meegan Earl, Vicki Fernandez, Beverly DeDonatis, Loretta and Gary Beasley, Barbara and Jose Carrera and Ed Muranaka, our tasters and critics; and Anne Bradford and Rose Mary Popp for their professional assistance. Special thanks to Rayne Pang for his support.

PART ONE
INFORMATION

WHY BE CONCERNED ABOUT YOUR BONES?

Overview

Osteoporosis has been known as a disease since the nineteenth century. Even then it was apparent that elderly women had an increased risk of long bone fractures after even minor falls. However, postmenopausal oestrogen deficiency was not linked to this disease until early in the twentieth century. How this protective effect of oestrogen works is unknown. It is thought to be indirect, probably through effects on other hormones. It is only recently, within the last few decades, that we have become aware that several other hormones—progesterone, androgens, PTH and so on—are also involved in a less significant though still important manner.

What exactly is osteoporosis? In medical terms, it is the ongoing loss of calcium from bones—osteopenia—that occurs as a normal part of the process of ageing. It happens to all of us to a greater or lesser degree, male or female. Osteopenia is a universal phenomenon; the cause of this age-related bone loss is not understood completely. It is important to differentiate osteopenia, a loss of bone density, from osteoporosis, the disease that results from this decreased density. Bone loss is obviously a complex process, the consequence of a negative net bone balance (less new bone being built while old bone continues to be lost at the usual rate). The process seems to involve alterations in the metabolism due to hormonal changes of ageing that interact with bone minerals.

Let us discuss what bone is so that we can have a better idea of what is happening. Bone consists of an organic matrix made up of collagen (strong semi-elastic protein fibres that hold body parts together) and noncollagen proteins, impregnated with calcium and phosphorus. There are two major forms of bone. The outer shell (cortical bone) of a long bone, necessary for support, is strong and compact. This outer part makes up 80 per cent of the bone. The inner part of a bone (trabecular bone) is made up of a series of porous interconnected plates; it is here that the blood vessels and marrow reside. The amount of each kind of bone varies in different bones—spine bones are predominantly trabecular while hip bones have more cortical bone. This difference results in a dissimilar response to the various metabolic influences and a disparate chance of fracture.

Several hormones are involved in the development and maintenance of bone. These include vitamin D (which in spite of its name is not a vitamin, but a hormone), which is made in the skin or ingested in food. This important hormone allows the absorption of dietary calcium and has several other metabolic functions relative to bone augmentation.

Calcium accumulates in bones up to approximately age twenty-five. Over the next decade the amount of bone calcium remains fairly stable. Starting at about thirty-five years of age, a natural, gradual loss of calcium begins. Bone loss occurs at the rate of approximately 3 per cent per decade, starting in the mid-thirties. This loss continues slowly; in women, at the time of menopause (either natural or surgically induced), a marked acceleration of bone loss occurs, lasting approximately five to seven years. Bone loss then slows down somewhat, but may continue at a rate of up to 9 per cent per decade until the seventies, then returning to a more gradual loss until the late seventies, at which time it becomes imperceptible.

Osteopenia takes place in both sexes, but becomes a problem significantly later in males because men start with a greater bone density. This is probably related to their greater intake of calcium in their teens and twenties, as well as the greater amount of physical activity that they usually undertake. The male hormone testosterone also plays an ill-defined role. Therefore it takes longer to reach a critically low mass. It is apparent that the risk of developing osteoporosis in adult life depends on bone mass at maturity.

As we gain more knowledge, it is evident that osteoporosis is not a single disease, but can be separated into several types, differentiated on the basis of fracture patterns and age when bone loss begins. Type I (post-menopausal) osteoporosis most frequently occurs in the trabecular bone of the spine in women aged fifty-five to seventy-five and results in vertebral fractures. Type II (involutional or senile) osteoporosis usually results in hip fractures in both sexes at an older age and involves the loss of both kinds of bones. Having one type of osteoporosis does not necessarily indicate the presence of the other. Since osteoporosis is a silent disease, we will not know of its presence until a fracture or deformity, with or without trauma, appears. In order for a break to occur, the trauma may be of only minimal degree.

Who is likely to get osteoporosis? If a typical patient can be described, *she* would be a northern European Caucasian over the age of fifty. Blacks are much less prone to problems than are whites. This is certainly due to the fact that blacks start out with denser bones at any age, compared to non-blacks, for unknown reasons. For this same reason, European (and probably Asian) women are at higher risk than African-origin females. The risk for the Latino and other populations at this time is unknown.

In a typical Caucasian ethnic group, 50 per cent of women over age sixty-five will have wedging of the spine—the rectangular bone will be partially collapsed and will develop a triangular shape. This effect shows a steady increase with age. A complete break will cause the spinal bones to look like pancakes. These compression fractures will occur in 10 per cent of Caucasian women by age sixty-five and in 20 per cent by age seventy. In addition, and more serious, 15 per cent will experience hip fracture over their lifetime, with a 2 per cent chance of hip fracture for each year after eighty. Additionally, 15 per cent will have wrist fractures, which can be severely disabling in an elderly individual who may already have significant problems with arthritis. Is this due to genetic, nutritional, environmental or constitutional causes? The question is currently under intensive investigation in the hope that the answer may give medical science a better handle on prevention and treatment.

Thin individuals are known to be more prone to problems than the overweight. This is probably because of their smaller bone mass; they reach the theoretical fracture threshold faster. The protective effect of obesity is due to the oestrogen production that occurs in fat tissue. (This may be the only truly beneficial effect of obesity. Overweight women are, however, at substantially greater risk of uterine cancer because of excess oestrogen.) Early menopause or surgical removal of the ovaries without replacement oestrogen treatment is also a known cause of osteoporosis. There is some suggestive information indicating that pregnancy and breast-feeding may have a limited protective effect. The reasons for this are entirely unknown.

Men indeed also have an increased risk of osteoporotic fractures, though starting at a significantly later age because of their higher baseline bone density. The overall chance for men of all ages of having a hip or wrist fracture over their lifetime is less than 5 per cent. This is also true of black men or women. This sex difference in bone loss is poorly understood. Be that as it may, the most common fracture in men is that of the hip, followed next by shoulder and pelvis breaks, while in women the most common site is the wrist, then the spine, and then the shoulder, hip and pelvis in that order. Sex and weight are only two considerations in bone loss. Other contributing factors include a positive family history; low muscle mass resulting from excessive exercise—muscle mass and muscle activity are correlated with a greater local bone mass until a certain level of exercise is surpassed, and at that point additional activity is unhealthy; the use of diet pills; lack of sunlight, especially in cloudy and overcast countries such as England, and among the frequently home-bound elderly, because of the decreased production of vitamin D in the skin; low-calcium diets, as exemplified by the minimal calcium-containing foods in the typical teenager's diet. Evidence suggests the requirements for calcium may actually *increase* with age. A somewhat speculative association is with high-protein diets, which are associated with high loss of calcium in urine. This may be why Eskimos, who eat protein-rich foods, are found to have a high rate of osteoporosis, in spite of their high intake of vitamin D.

The disease of osteoporosis has its onset in the sixth decade for women and the eighth decade for men. The most prominent factors for its onset at this time include lack of exercise, decreased oestrogen for any reason including excessive exercise, prolonged bed rest and inadequate calcium intake as a youth. The use of several different medications as well as non-medical substances also plays a very significant role. Such drugs as glucocorticoids (cortisone-like substances) block calcium uptake by bones. One of these is Prednisone, which at a relatively low dose of 7.5 mg per day can lead to fractures, especially of the ribs and spine, and degenerative changes in the hip, necessitating total hip replacement.

Nicotine from smoking leads to less dense bones partly because smokers tend to be thinner than non-smokers and women smokers undergo menopause earlier (for some women maybe this is a benefit of smoking?); in addition, nicotine has a yet undetermined direct effect on bone metabolism. Other frequently used dietary components that contribute to a significantly increased risk of developing the disease are caffeinated drinks including coffee and colas, which are becoming arch enemies of good health, and the known toxic chemical alcohol. Heparin, a drug used to dissolve blood clots, and methotrexate, a frequently used anti-cancer medication that is now being used for other chronic degenerative diseases, are also known culprits.

Several less documented causes for osteoporosis include high-protein diets (possibly because more calcium is bound, preventing its absorption); and poorly controlled diabetes mellitus, which is associated with an increased ankle fracture rate, rather uncommon in the non-diabetic. Rheumatoid arthritis may also be a cause, possibly secondary, as a result of treatment with cortisone-like drugs. It is interesting to note that osteoporosis is not increased in osteo-arthritis, a much more commonly encountered joint problem; in actual fact, it may be decreased.

A serious cause of osteoporosis is the use of thyroid hormone in greater than replacement doses; like the disease of hyperthyroidism, this may lead to excessive loss of bone. It is critical that early treatment be instituted because once the bone is lost, there is no return of this lost bone. It is now standard practice to get patients out of bed as soon after surgery as possible, since immobilization leads rapidly, after only a few weeks, to consequential bone loss.

Osteomalacia, the effect of vitamin D deficiency on bones, in the elderly is frequently associated with osteoporosis because of vitamin D deficiency from low intake, low sun exposure, deficiency in metabolism from liver or kidney disease, alcoholism and use of some antacids that bind phosphate. These usually contain aluminium, and it is important to be aware of this since the ingestion of antacids is very common in the elderly. Fortunately, a deficit of vitamin D is easily treatable with supplements.

The following diseases or disorders are also associated with increased bone-thinning and risk of fracture: Cushing's syndrome, from excess cortisone production; prolactin excess due to either a tumour or pituitary overactivity; chronic alcoholism; cirrhosis; primary hyperparathyroidism; plasma-cell dyscrasia (a type of blood cell cancer); leukaemia; carcinomatosis (widespread cancer metastasis); scurvy (vitamin C deficiency); chronic obstructive pulmonary disease (COPD), which is probably secondary to smoking; acromegaly; lactose intolerance. Other as yet unknown nutritional deficiencies or genetic diseases

may also play a role.

It has been noted that the jaw is often involved in osteopenia and osteoporosis. Dentists have noted for years that there is an increased tooth loss with ageing. This is not unexpected, but what has recently been found is that the greater the loss of calcium from the spine, the greater the number of teeth lost. A fracture of the wrist is the most common fracture prior to seventy-five years of age. Though there is rarely a need for hospitalization, significant discomfort and disability do occur, often resulting in the temporary need for help with the normal activities of daily living until healing has taken place. Under these circumstances, the repair process is often prolonged; and of course we can't forget the cost of additional nursing care or the mental stress of having an elderly, semi-helpless parent move in. These social and practical problems also arise if the broken bone is the humerus (the bone in the upper arm from shoulder to elbow).

Fractures of the spine or hip are often problematical for many years and may even contribute to the death of the victim. The frequency of collapse of the spine is unknown; however, by the age of seventy, 5 per cent of women will have had frank symptoms. Astoundingly, close to 100 per cent of women over the age of eighty will have X-ray evidence of collapse resulting in an often significant loss of height. These fractures may occur spontaneously or after only minimal trauma such as coughing or bending or lifting. Often there are no symptoms. With the accumulation of several fractures, a round back deformity or dowager's hump, of the mid to upper spine may become prominent, as does the obvious decrease in stature. This injury regularly leads to weeks or months of acute pain, and many years of disabling chronic back pain. The earliest suggestion that a problem may be imminent is the asymptomatic wedging seen on a routine chest or abdomen X-ray or the obvious shrinkage in height.

The hip (projection formed by the pelvis and the upper part of the thigh bone) is the site of the most devastating of all fractures. Hip fracture is the most common fracture after the age of seventy-five and the frequency is expected to double or treble by the year 2050. This growth is due to the increasing number of the elderly as a percentage of the population. Seventy-five per cent of these fractures will occur in women, half of them in the over-eighty age group. In the over-ninety population, a third of all women and a sixth of all men will break their hip.

The tragedy of all this is that these often previously productive individuals have a 12-20 per cent greater risk of dying in the next year than individuals of the same age with other fractures. The expected risk of death is only about 9 per cent, but it becomes progressively worse with increasing age at the time of fracture. From sixty to sixty-nine years of age, the post-fracture death rate is 8.6 per cent with an expected rate of 2 per cent; at seventy to seventy-nine years, 13.9 per cent (expected 5 per cent); at eighty to eighty-nine years, 20.7 per cent (expected 11 per cent). Overall, 50 per cent of persons sustaining a hip fracture will be dead in three years. So far we have just mentioned the medical aspects of this treacherous disease. In more personal terms it is known that for those who were living independently at home prior to the fracture, 25 per cent will remain in a long-term nursing care facility for more than one year; and that half who are able to go home will need help and/or devices to allow them to walk and enable them to recover some portion of their independence. It has also become apparent that there is a better one-year survival rate after hospital discharge for those who are better able to ambulate. The survival rate is 93.3 per cent if a walking frame is needed, 73.4 per cent if the patient is confined in a wheelchair, and a dismal 31.5 per cent if the patient is bedridden. Survival is also improved, the faster it takes to get surgical intervention for broken hips under way—91 per cent if the surgery is performed in the first twenty-four hours and only 83 per cent if undertaken after twenty-four hours.

A proper evaluation for osteoporosis should consist of a complete history and physical exam, several specific and general blood tests and an evaluation of spine and/or hip bone density by one of several new scanning methods—qualitative X-ray (QCT) or x-ray beam photon absorptiometry (DEXA). The latter means is more suitable for following the effects of therapy since the amount of radiation compared to QCT is minimal.

Now let us look at the areas of prevention, education and treatment.

PREVENTION OF BONE LOSS AND BONE INJURY

Prevention is a two-pronged matter: preventing osteoporosis and preventing fracture and/or disability once osteoporosis has occurred. Prevention is the most effective treatment since, once significant osteoporosis has occurred, means of treatment other than oestrogen seem to be of little or no efficacy.* Therefore it is incumbent on all of us, men and women alike, to do everything possible to increase the maximal amount of bone calcium—prior to menopause in women and, even more important, prior to the age of thirty-five in both sexes. This can be done by maintaining an appropriate diet, exercise regimen and life-style.

Central to avoiding osteoporosis are the use of calcium and an active exercise plan. We should be taking in at least 1,000 mg of elemental calcium daily (and maybe even twice that)† and do thirty minutes non-stop exercise of a moderately energetic activity at least five days out of each week.

For those individuals in jeopardy, the best prevention of injury is to injury-proof their residences. Safety training to prevent falls in the elderly is absolutely critical, since 90 per cent of hip, forearm and pelvis fractures in the over-seventy-five age group in the United Kingdom occur from a fall. Each year almost one-third of persons over the age of sixty-five have a fall; and 2 per cent of all elderly persons seek medical care for treatment of falls, a very expensive proposition indeed!

The concept of risk-proofing living spaces is really a matter of common sense; proper placement of electrical cords, removal of loose throw rugs, use of railings on stairs, rubberized bathmats, adequate lighting and, of great importance, corrective lenses. Many individuals let their vanity interfere with their common sense and neglect to wear the spectacles they need to see with; con-

* *Editor's note:* Although several new drugs seem to have produced very encouraging results.

† *Editor's note:* Although the recommended dietary intake of calcium in the UK is 500 mg for adults (slightly more for children and teenagers) many experts feel this is far too low, and should be increased to 1000 mg as it is in North America.

sequently they run into or trip over objects they cannot see. (Beware of bifocals and lenses for cataracts, which may actually impede vision.) Other considerations include the placement of cupboards in kitchens, bathrooms and other rooms, at a level that does not put the individual in a precarious balance. Chairs and beds should be at a height that allows easy access. Even shoes or slippers of an improper style or fit can cause falls. The safest footwear is the modern running shoe. Slippers should fit snugly around the entire foot and not just slip over the toes.

When an illness occurs, prolonged bed rest should be strongly discouraged; hospitalized patients should be mobilized as soon as possible. It is interesting to note that osteoporosis occurs in astronauts because of their protracted lack of weight-bearing. Another effect of illness that is often not considered, especially in the elderly, involves the side-effects of medications. Recent evidence is very clear that sedative drugs such as tranquillizers, anti-depressants and anti-psychotics markedly increase the risk in the elderly of falling and causing bone breakage. Another commonly used group of medications that can cause problems with stability are the anti-hypertensives. These blood pressure-lowering drugs may be 'too effective' in the aged person: they may lead to too low a blood pressure, especially when the user is standing, and may cause dizziness or fainting spells and may result in falls and fractures.

Of course the most critical part of prevention is the education of the teenage girl and, even before that, her parents. Certainly males also need this, but because of the innate differences between the sexes, little additional counselling needs to be done in the area of dietary calcium intake.

The two critical areas of education are exercise and diet. In both of these, females of all ages are generally deficient. The tugging on the bones during physical activity causes localized electrical currents and pressures that are immensely important in ensuring maximal bone density before age twenty-five. However, too much exercise is as bad as no exercise at all. When a woman's activity level is high and her total body fat is low, as occurs in ballet dancers, swimmers, long-distance runners, among others, her oestrogen level falls and her period stops; this is very much akin to what happens during menopause. Fortunately, as recent preliminary evidence suggests, decreasing activity and/or increasing body fat will allow partial catch-up deposition of calcium in bones.

In our very fast-paced lives we tend to neglect proper eating; and nowhere is this truer than in the pre-teen and teenage female. A fast burger here, with a lunch consisting of a bag of crisps; no food for three days to be able to wear the form-fitting party dress—we have all seen this happen over and over again. One of the results is that young women get only half or less of the daily requirement of calcium, setting the invincible youth up for major traumas as a pretty vincible (as in visible and *in*visible) adult. Therefore it seems rational to supplement the diet of youths with calcium, either by convincing them of the importance of at least a pint of milk a day, or by adding high-calcium recipes to their diet at home. The *least* acceptable choice would be to add calcium pills to their daily intake. Supplements can be just another step toward forming the wrong attitude that taking a pill can cure or control everything. Pills may sometimes be necessary, but natural intake of calcium is certainly preferable.

Many senior schools have health education courses. This is the time and place to emphasize the need for exercise and proper diet. Indeed, it makes tremendous health and financial sense to start this type of education at an earlier age.

In summary, it should be obvious that prevention is the best current medicine. In lieu of that, however, for those of us, male and female, over thirty-five, the solution is to exercise safely and in moderation for thirty minutes at least five days a week and to indulge ourselves in one or more of the wonderfully exciting and bone-maintaining recipes that now await you. Go to it with vim and vigour and keep those bones strong.

CALCIUM: THE SIMPLE FACTS

'*A calcium pill a day keeps the doctor away.*' A new twist to an old saying reflects popular thinking about calcium and bone health. But is that all there is to it? The flood of recent research on this topic suggests not. In this chapter the dietary aspects of osteoporosis will be reviewed, including calcium sources and requirements, the effects of other nutrients on calcium utilization, and the latest news on calcium supplementation.

Calcium and the cow

No discussion of calcium can begin without mention of where this vital nutrient can be found. You undoubtedly know by now that milk and other dairy products are good sources of calcium; in fact, they are the primary suppliers of calcium to our diet. Not only do milk, cheese and yogurt provide 250 mg* of calcium or more per serving, more than almost any other food, but the combination of other nutrients—lactose, vitamin D, protein, phosphorus and magnesium, without fibre, sodium, phytate or oxalate—facilitates absorption of calcium like no other food. (Cream, soft cheese, butter and non-dairy substitutes like coffee creamers and frozen desserts contain very little or no calcium, however).

Other calcium-packed foods include mackerel, sardines and salmon with bones, smelts and tofu processed with calcium sulphate. Moderate sources of calcium include curd and cottage cheese, most shellfish, pulses (especially soya beans and haricot beans), almonds, Brazil nuts, hazelnuts, pak-choi, broccoli, greens (especially spring greens, cabbage, parsley, spinach and watercress) and dried apricots. For a complete list, see the appendix at the back of the book.

Editor's note: based on $\frac{1}{3}$ pint milk, 1 oz cheese, 5 oz yoghurt ie typical servings.

How much is enough?

The recommended daily intake for calcium is currently 600 mg for children and young adults, and 700 mg for nine to fourteen-year-olds and 1,200 mg for pregnant and lactating women. Recommendations have been made by numerous experts for increasing the allowance to 1,000 mg for men and pre-menopausal women, unless they are taking oestrogen.

These allowances assume an absorption rate of calcium through the intestinal tract of about 30 per cent, although this rate is affected by a number of factors, both nutritional and physiological. Calcium and phosphorus deficiency increase the absorption rate of calcium, but not enough to compensate for extremely low intakes. Many disease states and medications affect the absorption of calcium; some are reviewed elsewhere in this book. Epidemiologically speaking, age is probably the biggest factor for calcium utilization, however. Significantly more calcium is absorbed during high growth periods such as childhood, pregnancy and lactation, while the elderly and post-menopausal women absorb a smaller fraction of dietary calcium than do younger adults.

Calcium-nutrient interactions

Finally, as is the case with all nutrients, calcium absorption and use by the body depend on the form in which the calcium appears and the other foods with which it is eaten. Certain dietary components—fibre, lactose, vitamin D, caffeine and oxalic acid, to name a few—positively or negatively influence the amount of dietary calcium that can eventually be incorporated into bone. Protein and phosphorus are neutral as far as calcium utilization is concerned. The effects of sodium and some other nutrients have not clearly been established.

Two nutrients known to increase calcium absorption are lactose, found primarily in milk and milk products and vitamin D, found in fortified milk products, and oily fish. This is partly why dairy foods are first-stringers in terms of calcium contribution to our diet.

Lactose, or milk sugar, is found in large amounts in milk and soft cheeses (such as cottage cheese). In cultured dairy products such as hard cheese and yogurt, much of the lactose is converted to lactic acid by bacterial action, so the lactose content of

Calcium Utilization
The Effect of Dietary Components

Increase	Decrease	Neutral
lactose	fibre	phosphorus
vitamin D	phytic acid (minor)	fat
	oxalic acid	
	nicotine (smoking)	
	caffeine	
	excessive alcohol (long-term)	
	sodium (presumed)	
	protein	

these foods is reduced. Exactly how lactose facilitates calcium absorption is not known, but it may be related to the relatively slow rate of lactose absorption from the intestine. Glucose, a rapidly absorbed sugar, has been shown to have no effect on calcium absorption, while sorbitol actually decreases it.

Recent studies show that the calcium in dairy products is well-absorbed even in those who do not digest lactose or who drink milk with lactase, the enzyme that breaks down milk sugar, added to it. This is good news for the many adults who are lactose-intolerant. Symptoms that appear after ingesting milk sugar—cramping, gas, bloating—can often be avoided by taking small amounts of milk with other foods, by using Lactaid milk or adding LactAid tablets to milk, or by getting calcium from

yogurt and cheese. Knowing that the calcium in these foods will be well-absorbed makes the effort worthwhile.

Vitamin D is necessary for the absorption of calcium from the intestinal tract. It is found in milk (which is fortified with the vitamin), fatty fish, margarine, eggs and liver. Sunlight also transforms a vitamin D precursor to the active form in your skin. Between fifteen minutes and one hour of sun exposure a day will convert the vitamin D necessary to facilitate calcium absorption.

The production of vitamin D decreases in the elderly. Those confined indoors who also have a marginal food intake are especially prone to vitamin D deficiency. In such cases, vitamin D supplementation to the level of the recommended daily intake might be warranted. Breast milk is also low in vitamin D, and breast-fed infants are usually given supplements. In the healthy adult population, however, excess supplementation with vitamin D is unnecessary and may actually reduce calcium status. Excessive doses of this vitamin can damage the heart, kidney and arteries by calcification and should be avoided.

Along with calcium, fibre was certainly the 'newtrient' of the eighties. Its benefits with regard to cancer, diabetes, heart disease and constipation have been proclaimed only too well in advertisements, newspapers and magazines.

In spite of all the publicity, fibre is not the perfect food: in very large amounts it does reduce the absorption of calcium. In one study, doubling the fibre intake by substituting wheat flour and bran for white flour in a typical Western diet caused the subjects to go into negative calcium balance even though their calcium intake was high. In effect, the fibre bound about 110 mg of the calcium so that it was not absorbed. In another study, increasing fibre intake with the addition of fruits and vegetables to a normal diet increased calcium intake by about 100 mg. Even so, the subjects came up short on calcium because absorption was decreased by about 300 mg per day.

Fibre, also known as bulk or roughage, is not a single nutrient, but rather the umbrella term for a number of plant components resistant to digestion by the small intestine. The exact fibrous substance that inhibits calcium uptake is not known, but cellulose, pectin and uronic acid have all been implicated.

Cellulose, found in whole-grain products such as wholemeal bread and bran cereal, reduces calcium absorption to an unknown degree; research with pectin, found largely in fruits, has shown it to have a negligible effect. Uronic acid, present in cereals, fruits and vegetables, does bind calcium to a large extent, although most of the uronic acid in foods is broken down in the intestine, possibly releasing the calcium and making it available for absorption.

Phytic acid, a strong acid, combines with calcium and other minerals to form a salt, phytate, that cannot be absorbed. It is present in whole grains, bran, nuts and pulses. Phytate has long been held responsible for calcium imbalance and bone loss. In early-twentieth-century England, flour was supplemented with calcium carbonate as a way to reduce the incidence of rickets in children. The blame may have been misplaced, however. Phytate is broken down by bacteria and digestive enzymes in the intestine, as well as by yeast in bread and other leavened products, freeing the calcium for absorption. Evidence also exists that our bodies can adapt to a diet high in phytic acid after several weeks, resulting in an improved absorption rate for calcium. So while phytic acid does inhibit calcium absorption to some extent, its effect is probably minor, especially compared with fibre itself.

Oxalic acid is another plant substance that forms a salt (oxalate) with calcium in the intestine, presumably limiting its absorption. Since rhubarb, spinach and Swiss chard contain much more oxalic acid than calcium, it is believed that all of the calcium in these foods binds to oxalic acid and is therefore unavailable. More research needs to be done in this area, however. Whether the oxalic acid found in these vegetables and in sources such as peanuts, wheatgerm and tea binds calcium from other foods eaten at the same meal is also not known. Bacteria that degrade oxalic acid have been discovered in the intestinal tract of man, leaving open the possibility that calcium might be freed for absorption.

If you had given up your beloved chocolate milk after hearing that the oxalic acid in cocoa ties up its calcium, suffer no more. The oxalate content of chocolate milk is negligible, and this drink remains an excellent source of calcium for the chocolate lover.

Does all this talk about fibre and calcium mean that you should feed your bran to the birds and ransack your store cupboard for the familiar tin of peaches? Not yet. *Moderate* amounts—about 25 to 35 grams per day—eaten with a diet rich in calcium will provide you with the many—benefits of fibre, but won't significantly impair your calcium status.* This level of fibre intake can easily be achieved with whole grains, fruits and vegetables, but you can leave the bran supplements on the supermarket shelf and occasionally enjoy plain old white bread without guilt, if you please.

Unlike fibre, the remaining factors to be reviewed that impair calcium status—smoking, drinking caffeine, excessive alcohol and sodium use—have few, if any, redeeming qualities. Still, most of us cling to at least one of these habits and their effects on calcium deserve some discussion.

To the laundry list of dangers associated with cigarette smoking, you can add one more: an increased risk of osteoporosis. Smoking reduces oestrogen levels and contributes to an early menopause, followed by accelerated bone loss. Nicotine may also directly increase calcium excretion, and its effect may be related to the alcohol and caffeine consumption that often go hand in hand with smoking.

If you are hooked on that morning cup of coffee, try adding a little milk or dried milk powder for a calcium boost. Why? It has been found that 175 mg of caffeine—the amount in 8 fluid ounces of drip or percolated coffee—leads to a urinary calcium loss of 6 mg. This may not sound like much, but if you drink six or seven cups a day, you could lose enough calcium to make a noticeable difference in bone mass over the course of one year. Instant coffee, strong tea and cola drinks also contain caffeine, roughly 30 to 90 mg per cup or can. And don't forget the caffeine in non-prescription drugs, about 200 mg per dose of weight control, diuretic and stimulant pills, and 30 to 130 mg in pain and cold medications.

Like smoking and drinking coffee, there's not much good that can be said for drinking alcohol, and its effect on calcium is no exception. Chronic alcohol abuse leads to bone demineralization, even in young adults. Alcohol directly alters the intestinal lining, so that calcium is poorly absorbed.

* Editor's note: This would be considered high in the UK; NACNE has suggested 30 grams per day.

Additionally, alcoholics frequently have impaired liver and intestinal function and eat inadequate diets, leading to deficiencies in vitamin D and calcium.

Sodium has certainly taken a back seat to other seasonings on the shelves of savvy home and restaurant chefs. A link between sodium and calcium loss may be one reason why. Several studies suggest that excessive dietary sodium leads to an increase in urinary calcium loss, although it is too early to identify the levels of sodium and calcium intake at which this becomes significant.

Phosphorus, along with calcium, is a major mineral component of bone. It is readily available in our diet and can be found in generous amounts in milk, meat, poultry and fish. The recommended daily intake for phosphorus in the US is 800 mg per day for children and adults, and 1,200 mg for eleven- to eighteen-year-olds and pregnant and lactating women. The average daily intake in the US is between 800 and 1,200 mg, with higher intakes resulting from the heavy consumption of soft drinks, which can have up to 60 mg phosphorus per 12 fluid ounces.

For many years, on the basis of results from animal research, excessive dietary phosphorus was thought to have a negative impact on calcium balance and bone formation. Recent studies on humans, however, have concluded that phosphorus intakes as high as 2,000 mg per day have no adverse effect on calcium metabolism. In fact, the high phosphorus diet had the beneficial effect of decreasing urinary calcium excretion without decreasing calcium absorption. The results were consistent over a range of calcium intakes between 200 and 2,000 mg per day. But the phosphoric acid in soft drinks and the forms of phosphate added to processed foods may affect calcium balance differently from the phosphorus found naturally in food.

Like phosphorus, protein has been believed to increase calcium requirements, and consumers for years have been advised to limit the consumption of meat and other high-protein foods. Recent long-term studies with high-protein diets in the form of red meat as much as $1\frac{1}{4}$ pounds of meat taken per day—refute the earlier findings, however. The high-protein diets did not increase urinary calcium excretion, nor did they reduce the absorption of calcium or induce calcium loss. In the earlier studies, purified proteins were used, not actual dietary proteins such as meat, poultry, fish and dairy products. As previously discussed, these foods contain phosphorus, which appears to counteract the effect of the protein itself on calcium excretion.

What this means is that in terms of calcium nutrition, your consumption of meat and other high-protein foods does not need to be limited. It is true, though, that as sources of saturated fat, cholesterol and calories, animal proteins should be eaten in moderate amounts, approximately 5 to 8 ounces per day for the average healthy adult.

Finally, fat has been implicated as reducing calcium absorption because fatty acids—components of dietary fat—combine with calcium in the intestine, rendering it unabsorbable. This occurs only in people with malabsorption of fat (known medically as steatorrhea) and not in healthy people. Calcium absorption has been shown to be unaffected by even relatively large amounts of dietary fat in healthy volunteers. Even so, a high-fat diet is associated with heart disease, obesity and an increased risk of some types of cancer, so a prudent diet with no more than 25 to 30 per cent of total calories coming from fat is recommended.

As you have seen, there are many dietary and related factors contributing to calcium balance and bone density. But you don't need a computer programme to plan your menus; it's simpler than you might think:

1. Look to a variety of foods to meet your nutritional requirements. Relying on just a few foods—even healthy ones—can result in nutrient imbalances, such as the effects of too much fibre and oxalate on calcium. A varied diet helps to ensure that your body will be supplied with everything it needs. Remember, you *can* get too much of a good thing!

2. As sources of calcium, phosphorus, protein, vitamin D, lactose, magnesium, manganese and other important nutrients, dairy products should not be overlooked as major players in your diet plan. Aim for at least two to three servings per day, more if you are a teenager or if you are pregnant, lactating or at risk for osteoporosis.

3. If you drink large amounts of coffee, switch to de-caffeinated types, reduce your consumption, or add some milk for a calcium boost. Soft drinks and tea are probably best taken one hour before or several hours after high-calcium meals, to prevent possible calcium binding.

4. Give up cigarette smoking.

5. Avoid supplements of vitamin D, fibre, diuretics, diet pills, stimulants and other medication unless prescribed by your physician.

THE SUPPLEMENT STORY

If you're a woman and you ever watch television or read magazines, you've certainly seen the adverts that so graphically depict the pained, stooped, pathetic woman you will become if you fail to take a calcium supplement. You may even believe—and understandably so—that taking calcium supplements will ensure the arrival of your golden years with good posture and a healthy glow. On the other hand, if you have an above-average interest in health and nutrition, you may have read in recent magazine and newspaper columns that taking calcium supplements will not prevent osteoporosis and in fact may not have much benefit at all. Are you thoroughly confused yet?

Interest in calcium started in the US in 1984 after the American National Institutes of Health Consensus Conference on Osteoporosis. On the basis of research to date, the conference essentially concluded that the recommended daily intake for calcium should be raised from 800 mg per day for adults to 1,000 mg for men, pre-menopausal women and post-menopausal women on oestrogen. A recommended daily intake of 1,500 mg was recommended for post-menopausal women not on oestrogen, in whom calcium absorption is reduced and fracture risk is high. This started the bandwagon for supplementation, to the tune of $240 million in sales in the United States in 1986 alone.

Much research has been published in the area of calcium and bone density since then, quite a bit of it seeming to contradict earlier studies. It appears that younger women need a calcium intake of at least 1,000 mg per day to achieve calcium balance (the same amount of mineral going out of the body as coming in). But it has also been shown in several studies that a positive calcium balance—the condition that exists when more calcium is going into the body than is being excreted—for a period of two years did not result in denser bones on bone measurement tests, as would be expected. This suggests either that the calcium balance data was flawed or that calcium balance does not reflect bone density. Clearly, more research needs to be done in this area.

Likewise, it has yet to be proven that a high-calcium diet throughout life will prevent osteoporosis in later years. All we know for sure is that a deficiency of calcium will lead to bone loss. In a classic study comparing two Yugoslavian communities with similar ethnicity, level of activity and exposure to the sun, but with different calcium intakes, the high-calcium group (median intake of 900 mg per day) had greater bone mass and the seniors in that group experienced half as many fractures of the leg as the seniors in the low-calcium group (median of 400 mg per day). However, the metacarpal bone densities of the two groups by the time they reached the age of sixty-five were nearly identical.

Some studies have shown increases in hand bone density following calcium supplementation in elderly osteoporosis patients, and others show a slowed loss of at least one type of bone, after calcium supplementation of 800 to 1,000 mg per day for post-menopausal women.

Still other researchers had quite different results. Riis and others at the University of Copenhagen compared bone densities for several body sites over a two-year period in forty-three women in their early post-menopausal years. Those taking 2,000 mg calcium daily had a slightly slowed loss of dense bone in the body compared with women taking a placebo, but bone losses from the spine and parts of the forearm were similar. Only women in the oestrogen-treated group retained their bone mass. In other words, even the large doses of calcium taken did little to arrest bone loss in this population. It appears, however, that 1,500 mg calcium taken daily along with .3 mg oestrogen—half the usual dose—does slow post-menopausal bone loss or even increases bone mass of the spongy trabecular bone.

What does all this mean? Part of the confusion stems from the fact that the researchers measured various types of bones and tested bone densities at different post-menopausal ages. Trying to compare the data from two studies, then, may be like comparing *The Financial Times* and *Homes and Gardens*: both are valid sources, but each gives you completely different information.

In the studies that have been done, two different types of bone have been measured: dense cortical bone and spongy trabecular bone. If the hand or upper part of the forearm is tested for bone loss, cortical bone is measured. When the spine, wrist or part of the forearm near the wrist is tested, primarily trabecular bone is measured. The two types of bones differ in composition and in rate of loss. Cortical bone is lost at a rapid rate just after menopause, while spongy bone is lost at a steady rate after the age of thirty. Calcium affects the loss of dense bone, but not the softer bone of the wrist and spine; therefore, results of a research study depend on where the bone is measured, at what point in menopause the tests are conducted. If cortical bone is measured, especially if it is just before menopause or after the age of seventy, the effect of calcium supplementation on bone density will be much more favourable than if spongy bone is measured during the immediate post-menopausal years.

This all boils down to the following:

• Calcium supplementation cannot be said to prevent osteoporosis, especially if it is delayed until menopausal years.

• Adequate calcium intake (approximately 1,000 mg per day) throughout life will at least reduce the risk of fracture of dense bone, such as the leg, hip, hand and upper forearm bones.

• The effectiveness of calcium supplementation in post-menopausal women is greatly increased by the addition of small amounts of oestrogen.

So you know that you need to get enough calcium in your diet: between 1,000 and 1,500 mg per day, depending on your stage in life. You know that popping calcium pills is not a panacea for osteoporosis. You even know that other foods and substances that you ingest will affect your calcium balance and bone integrity. So now what do you do?

First, take a good look at your current diet. It might be helpful to write down everything that you eat for three to five days, including Saturday and/or Sunday. Count how many high-calcium foods you eat per day. High calcium sources are those providing about 250 mg calcium in one serving. A third of a pint of milk or a 5 oz tub of yogurt, 1 ounce of hard cheese (not cottage cheese) and 7 oz of pudding made with milk all qualify, as do 2 oz of sardines, 4 oz of tofu, 3 stalks of fresh broccoli and 1 large serving of cooked spring greens.

How many high-calcium servings would you have received if this had been your menu for one day?

You would have eaten the equivalent of

	Menu	High calcium sources
Breakfast:	4 fl oz milk	$\frac{1}{2}$
	1 oz corn flakes	
	6 fl oz orange juice	
Lunch:	Chefs salad with cheese and blue cheese dressing	1 or more
	bread roll with butter	
	diet soft drink	
Snack:	apple	
Dinner:	3 ounces baked chicken	1
	baked potato with soured cream	
	5 oz frozen broccoli	
	4 oz cup pudding	
	tea with milk	
Snack:	3 oz cottage cheese	
	3 tbsp raisins	

over two high calcium sources, providing about 500 mg calcium. The next step is to identify other calcium sources in your diet. Refer to the appendix, Food Sources of Calcium, pages 139-142 for assistance. For the sample day, other calcium sources include the serving of broccoli at dinner and the 3 oz of cottage cheese in the evening, for about 125 mg added calcium. Although broccoli can be a major source of calcium, the portion in the sample menu was small and came from frozen, so it contributed only about 50 mg to the day's total.

You don't actually need to add up the exact calcium contribution from these medium sources, but rather get a general idea of whether or not it is significant. If you regularly eat foods that contain some calcium, like prawn salad, cream soup and frozen yogurt, for example, your calcium total could be raised by 300 mg or more per day. If most of these foods are only occasionally or never eaten, however, the daily calcium contribution would average under 100 mg.

Once you've estimated the calcium in your diet from high and medium food sources, you can add 50 to 100 mg to account for the small amount of calcium from the remaining foods in your diet. Then compare this total to your calcium requirement. (Remember, at least 1,000 mg is thought necessary for healthy adults, with 1,200 mg required for teenagers and pregnant and lactating women).* In the sample menu above, about 800 mg of calcium was eaten from all sources.

Shortfalls in your calcium intake should first be corrected by improving your diet. This is preferable to popping calcium pills because other nutrients in the food you eat will facilitate calcium utilization. Additionally, calcium in supplement form may inhibit the absorption of other essential nutrients like manganese, and at least a few experts are concerned about possible long-term side effects from large doses of the substances that carry the calcium in supplements.

The ways to increase the calcium in your diet are limited only by your imagination and sense of adventure. Can you make a point of drinking milk with your toast in the morning, or adding a quick breakfast milkshake if you usually run out with nothing in your stomach? The calorie content is a poor excuse for not drinking milk; skimmed milk has only 80 calories per 8 fluid ounces—less than the amount in one average sweet biscuit—and the calories are well-spent. If you don't like milk plain, try flavouring it with chocolate. Look for sugar-free brands at the supermarket to avoid the extra calories, if desired.

Cheese is a high-calcium substitute for

* UK Editor's note: In UK equivalents this would be, in UK terms, 500 mg for healthy adults, 600-700 mg for teenagers and 1,200 mg for pregnant and lactating women.

meat in sandwiches, with one of the reduced-fat varieties a good choice if fat or calories are a concern. Feta cheese is a tasty addition to tossed salads, as are tofu, anchovies and chick peas. All are good calcium sources. Many other ideas can be found in the recipe section of this book and on the Top Ten Tips list, page 40.

How can the calcium in the sample menu be increased? Adding another 4 fl oz of milk at breakfast, substituting soured cream with seasoned natural yogurt on the potato and having figs or dried apricots instead of raisins with the cottage cheese snack would bring the calcium total over 1,000 mg without increasing the calories. So would switching the cottage cheese to 1 ounce of cheddar cheese and adding more broccoli or another vegetable, such as a cos lettuce salad at dinner.

After you develop some strategies for getting more calcium in your diet, again compare your calcium intake to the recommended level. If your intake still falls short, you can make up the difference with a calcium supplement.

People who can't drink milk often question me about taking a calcium supplement. Even if you are lactose-intolerant, supplementation is not the immediate solution; you *can* get adequate amounts of calcium in your diet. Lactose—milk sugar—is usually broken down by an enzyme called lactase into two smaller sugars, glucose and galactose, which

are then absorbed. Lactose-intolerants have insufficient amounts of lactase, so bacteria in the intestines act on the milk sugar, forming lactic acid and gases, which lead to a bloated feeling, gas, cramping and diarrhoea. Many people with lactose intolerance can drink small amounts of milk with meals, however, without the unpleasant symptoms. Others use Lactaid milk or add LactAid, lactase in tablet form, to their milk. Such preparations break down the lactose without affecting the milk's calcium content. Since most of the lactose is broken down to lactic acid in cultured dairy products such as buttermilk, hard cheese, yogurt and frozen yogurt, these foods are usually well tolerated—contrary to popular opinion—except in the most severe cases.

If you are lactose-intolerant, try taking smaller amounts of the lactose-containing foods—milk, cottage cheese and other soft cheeses, ice cream—as part of your meal. Rely on cultured dairy products and other high-calcium foods like tofu, broccoli and salmon to boost your calcium intake. Many of the recipes in this book, like the Tofu Shake and Salmon-Tofu Patties, are made without dairy products.

Many questions come to mind when calcium supplementation is considered. How much to take? What kind? When during the day? First, supplements are meant to do just what they say—*supplement* your diet, not replace foods in it. The amount that you need to take depends on how much calcium you're getting from the food you eat, as well as other factors. For example, kidney-stone formers should probably not take supplements at all, because the calcium is not conserved normally and will end up in the urine, increasing the risk for calcium oxalate stone formation. (There is no conclusive evidence to support a low-calcium diet, however, and it may lead to bone loss. Kidney stones are probably most effectively treated with medication rather than by diet.)

When deciding which supplement would be most appropriate for you, look at the milligram amount of elemental calcium rather than the tablet size. If you are going to be taking a large dose, the calcium will be better utilized and probably better tolerated if you divide the dose and take two or three smaller pills throughout the day, rather than one large one.

There are many acceptable supplements available on the market. Calcium carbonate has the highest percentage of elemental calcium—40 per cent—so fewer pills are needed compared with other forms. It is also the least expensive form of supplement, especially the generic products.

When you swallow a tablet, it must disintegrate and then dissolve in your stomach before the calcium can be absorbed. Chewing a supplement increases its surface area and may enhance the absorption. Calcium carbonate needs an acid environment to dissolve, and many brands do not dissolve well, especially in older people and others with decreased gastric acidity.

If you have achlorhydria—impaired gastric acid secretion—take your supplement with meals. The food itself will generate enough acid to break down the calcium carbonate. The supplement chart includes calcium carbonate products that will be at least 75 per cent dissolved within thirty minutes after being swallowed. Supplements in liquid form are also available.

Some manufacturers claim that it is better to take your calcium with added vitamin A and/or vitamin D. Since both A and D can be toxic in large doses and because evidence shows that calcium is better utilized if taken alone, leave those preparations on the shop shelf. Vitamins A and D are readily available in foods and multivitamin preparations, and the sun converts vitamin D in our skin to the active form. Likewise, there is no evidence for taking other minerals, such as magnesium, with your calcium supplement. Two calcium preparations—dolomite and bone meal—should be avoided because of possible lead contamination. Oyster-shell calcium, on the other hand, is calcium carbonate and is perfectly safe.

Calcium tablets are generally best taken with meals. Some experts suggest taking your supplement before bedtime, to suppress calcium removal from bone at night. This theory has yet to be tested, however. If you develop stomach pain, gas, bloating or other symptoms after ingesting the supplement,

Acceptable calcium supplements

Name	Form	Calcium per tablet (mg)
Calcium Factor	carbonate	500
Calcia	carbonate	750
Seven Seas Calcium Berries	carbonate	500
Sanatogen Multi-vits plus calcium	tricalcium diorthophosphate	92
Unichem Multi-vits	not specified	100
Tums	carbonate	500
Rennies	carbonate	680

try taking it with meals, preferably dairy products. This should alleviate or reduce the symptoms, and the vitamin D and lactose in milk products will facilitate absorption of the calcium. Taking the supplement in smaller doses may also be beneficial.

EATING FOR BETTER BONES

There is much yet to be discovered about calcium, bone health and osteoporosis prevention. But not having all the answers should not prevent you from practising what will increase your chances of having strong, healthy bones throughout life. Most of the dietary recommendations in this book have numerous other health benefits. The very fact that the many reasons and ways to stay healthy and fit reinforce each other tends to verify their validity. To summarize what has been covered in detail already and what you can do for better bones:

• Enjoy a variety of foods, including dairy products and other high-calcium sources. Don't go overboard with fibre, or with those foods high in oxalic acid—spinach, rhubarb and Swiss chard. Moderation regarding sodium, alcohol and caffeine consumption is a good idea. Quit smoking.

• Avoid unnecessary supplementation with vitamin A, vitamin D, calcium, fibre and other vitamin-mineral preparations and over-the-counter drugs. They usually do more harm than good.

• If you can't squeeze in at least 1,000 mg of calcium per day on the average, a calcium supplement can bring you up to the desired level. Choose one that is readily dissolvable and convenient and of the appropriate dosage for your needs. Before bedtime or when eating dairy foods are the best times for supplementation. If you are getting close to the recommended daily intake for calcium in your diet and are otherwise at low risk for developing osteoporosis (you have a large bone structure; are active, healthy, non-Caucasian; have no family history; and so on), supplementation is probably not indicated.

• Walk, run, play tennis, squash, volley ball, basketball, whatever: exercise! Activities that put weight on your muscles and bones through the force of gravity are best, but all forms of exercise are beneficial.

• When you reach menopause, discuss with your doctor the pros and cons of hormone replacement therapy in your particular situation. There are many factors involved in deciding to take oestrogen or not, but taking it is the most effective way at present to arrest post-menopausal bone loss.

Top Ten Tips for Boosting Your Bone Calcium

1. Add 55-85g (2-3 oz) skimmed milk powder to recipes for scones, breads, mashed potatoes, scrambled eggs, puddings, biscuits, cakes and other foods. The milk powder can be blended into the other dry ingredients (flour, sugar, etc.) or added along with the water or liquid milk.

2. Substitute yogurt for soured cream in Beef Stroganoff, gelatine desserts, dips, dressings and toppings.

3. Choose spinach, cos lettuce and other brightly coloured salad greens instead of iceberg lettuce.

4. Use milk or buttermilk instead of water to reconstitute tinned soups, hot breakfast cereals, instant mashed potatoes and prepared salad dressings.

5. When feeding your sweet tooth, think calcium as well as calories. Pudding, frozen yogurt, ice milk and custard pack lots of nutritional bang for the calorie.

6. You can make your own 'double-strength' milk cheaply by adding skimmed milk powder to the regular milk you buy. Blending in 1 oz milk powder for each 8 fl oz of liquid milk will double the calcium content and make the milk richer without altering the taste.

7. Substitute half the mayonnaise in salad dressings and dips with natural yogurt. Dry soup or salad dressing mix can be added to liven up the flavour, if desired.

8. Lighten your coffee by adding milk or evaporated milk instead of cream. Or, for convenience, use skimmed milk powder rather than non-dairy creamer. *Cream and cream substitutes are loaded with fat and calories, but are poor calcium sources.*

9. Mix lemon juice, a few drops of olive oil, crushed garlic and grated Parmesan cheese for a low-calorie, high-calcium salad dressing.

10. Top casseroles, omelettes, toast, baked potatoes and steamed vegetables with shredded Cheddar, Emmenthal or mozzarella cheese for a tasty calcium boost.

Menu suggestions for the calcium-conscious diner

There are many restaurant menu items that are high in calcium; a few suggestions are listed below. To reduce the calorie count, use as little salad dressing, butter, soured cream and cream sauce as possible. Seafood dishes are especially lean.

Starters
artichoke with lemon
crab cocktail
cream soups
French onion soup
globe artichoke with lemon
oysters on the half shell
potato skins with cheese
seafood or prawn salad
shrimp cocktail
steamed clams

Beverages
Tia Maria and milk
low-fat or skimmed milk
milkshake

Continental dishes
cheese crépe
cheese omelette
Chef's salad (greens, cheese, ham, tongue)
chicken Cordon Bleu
chilli
peasant lunch (cheese cubes, fresh fruit, bread)
quiche
salad with dark greens, fresh vegetables, cheeses and chick peas or kidney beans
sandwiches made with cheese or meat and cheese
steamed vegetable plate with cheese sauce

Italian dishes
antipasto salad
aubergine parmigiana
Caesar salad
cheese pizza with anchovies
lasagne
linguine with white clam sauce
tortellini stuffed with ricotta cheese
veal parmigiana
other meat and cheese or pasta and cheese combinations

Oriental dishes
bean curd (tofu) dishes
beef with broccoli
prawns with black bean sauce
prawns with snow peas
sautéed broccoli or pak choi
scallops with bean curd
sweet and sour prawns
other prawn, scallop and lobster dishes

Seafood dishes
bouillabaisse
coquilles St.-Jacques
king crab

lobster tail
scampi
sole meunière
other shellfish dishes

A note on the recipes

The recipes in this book were designed with both your health and your palate in mind. They are, of course, rich in calcium from a variety of food sources, including dairy products, pulses, seafood, vegetables, fruits and nuts.

But they also follow current recommendations for the British diet. They are low in fat, moderate to high in fibre and complex carbohydrates and moderate in protein and sugar content. As an added benefit, the relatively low fat and sugar content of the recipes translates into dishes that are low in calories, especially compared to traditional recipes.

Since most modern cooks cannot afford to spend all day in the kitchen, the recipes were written to be as quick and convenient as possible without compromising taste, appeal or nutritional value.

42

PART TWO
RECIPES

STARTERS

Toasted Fish Canapés _____

Serves 6

100g (3½ oz) tinned sardines, packed in oil
¼ teaspoon Worcestershire sauce
¼ tablespoon finely chopped onion
1 tablespoon finely chopped parsley
2 tablespoons reduced-calorie mayonnaise
6 thin slices soft bread, white or wholemeal

1. Drain and mash sardines. Mix with
   Worcestershire sauce, onion, parsley and
   mayonnaise.
2. Remove the crusts from the bread. Spread
   with the sardine mixture.
3. Roll the slices and secure with cocktail
   sticks.
4. Toast under a hot grill immediately before
   serving, if desired.

Calories per serving: 100
Calcium per serving: 102mg

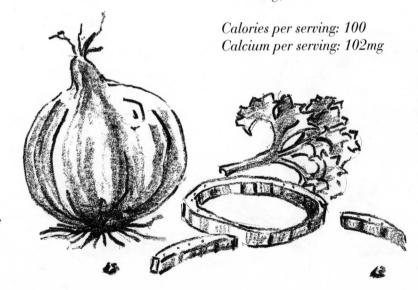

Lite and Lean Nachos

Special preparation methods result in nachos exceptionally low in fat but high in flavour.

Serves 4

6 x 15cm (6-inch) corn tortillas
vegetable oil
salt
420g (15 oz) tinned borlotti beans, drained
85g (3 oz) cheddar cheese, grated
2 small tomatoes, chopped
2 spring onions, chopped
60ml (2 fl oz) natural yogurt

1. Cut each tortilla into 6 wedges, like a pie. Spread out in a single layer on an ovenproof serving dish. Brush lightly with vegetable oil and sprinkle with salt.
2. Bake at 375°F (190°C/Gas Mark 5) for about 5 minutes. Turn wedges over and sprinkle with salt. Bake for a further 5 minutes, or until crisp.
3. Meanwhile, mash the borlotti beans and heat thoroughly over a moderate heat, stirring occasionally. Spread the tortilla wedges with the mashed beans and top with cheese.
4. Return tortillas to the oven and bake for a further 5 minutes, until cheese melts. Top with tomatoes, spring onions and yogurt.

Calories per serving: 288
Calcium per serving: 282mg

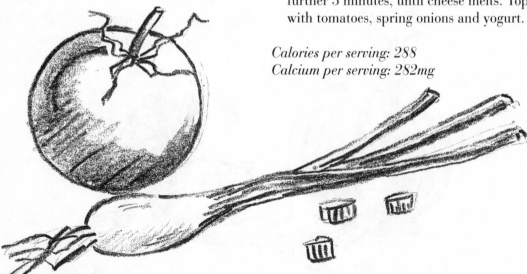

Salted Prawns

Delicious with a colourful tray of raw vegetables.

Serves 6

450g (1 lb) headless raw prawns, unshelled
2 tablespoons cornflour
240-360ml (8-12 fl oz) vegetable oil
  (enough almost to cover prawns)
1 teaspoon salt

1. Remove legs from prawns but do not remove shells. Rinse prawns thoroughly, drain and allow to dry in colander for about 15 minutes.
2. Place prawns in a bowl; add cornflour and mix to coat.
3. Heat the oil in a wok until very hot. Add the prawns and fry about 1 minute (until prawns just turn opaque).
4. Remove the prawns from the wok with a slotted spoon and drain on absorbent kitchen paper.
5. Remove oil from the wok (a light film will remain). Reheat wok over high heat; add prawns, then salt. Stir-fry for 45 seconds. Turn onto a heated serving plate and serve immediately.

Calories per serving: 134
Calcium per serving: 48mg

Seasoned Mozzarella Snacks

Makes 12 2-piece servings

225g (8 oz) low fat mozzarella cheese
2 eggs
1 tablespoon skimmed milk
85g (3 oz) dry breadcrumbs
2 teaspoons dried Italian seasoning, crushed
2 teaspoons garlic powder
1½ tablespoons chopped parsley
4 tablespoons unsifted plain flour

1. Cut cheese into 24 2.5cm (1-inch) cubes; set aside.
2. Prepare three shallow bowls; in the first, whisk the eggs together with the milk. Place the breadcrumbs, Italian seasoning, garlic powder and chopped parsley in the second bowl and combine well. Place the flour in the third bowl.
3. Coat the cheese completely with the flour, then the egg mixture and finally with the breadcrumb mixture.
4. Place the coated cheese in a single layer on a plate, cover with foil and refrigerate 2-3 hours or overnight.
5. Preheat the oven to 400°F (200°C/Gas Mark 6). Place cheese cubes on a foil-lined baking sheet and bake until crisp, 6-7 minutes. Let stand a few minutes before serving.

Calories per serving: 82 for 2 pieces
Calcium per serving: 149mg for 2 pieces

Stuffed Bread Rolls

Makes 12 2-slice servings

1 450g (1 lb) packet bread mix
1 bunch Swiss chard
85g (3 oz) cheddar cheese, grated
1 egg, beaten
2 tablespoons finely chopped onion
vegetable oil
1 tablespoon margarine
½ teaspoon garlic powder
2 tablespoons grated parmesan cheese

1. Make up the bread dough from the packet mix.
2. Cook the Swiss chard in 1-2 inches of boiling water in a covered saucepan for 15-20 minutes. Drain well and cool.
3. Mix the Swiss chard, cheddar cheese, egg and onion together.
4. Cut the bread dough in half. On a lightly floured board, roll out the dough into two 20 x 30cm (8 x 10-inch) rectangles.
5. Spread the Swiss chard mixture on the dough to within 2.5cm (1 inch) of the edges. Beginning with the long side, roll up tightly.
6. Lightly grease a baking sheet with the vegetable oil. Place the dough rolls on the sheet, seam side down. Melt the margarine and combine with the garlic powder and parmesan cheese. Brush on top of rolls. Let rolls rise until trebled in volume.
7. Preheat the oven to 375°F (190°C/Gas Mark 5). Bake for 25-30 minutes or until golden-brown. Cut each roll into 12 slices.

Calories per serving: 154 for 2 slices
Calcium per serving: 112mg for 2 slices

Classic Artichoke

The artichoke is simpler to prepare than you might think.

Serves 4

2 large globe artichokes
4-5 litres (8-10 pints) water
1 tablespoon olive oil
1½ tablespoons lemon juice
1 clove garlic, cut into quarters
½ teaspoon salt
reduced-calorie mayonnaise to serve

1. Remove any discoloured leaves and the small leaves from the base of the artichokes. Trim the stem even with the base. Cut off 2.5cm (1 inch) from the top of each artichoke and snip off the points of the leaves. Rinse well.
2. Heat the water in a large kettle. Add the lemon juice, garlic and salt and bring to the boil. Add the artichokes and bring to the boil again; reduce heat and simmer uncovered, rotating the artichokes occasionally until the leaves pull out easily, about 30-40 minutes.
3. When the artichokes are tender, remove from the kettle with kitchen tongs. Place upside down to drain.
4. Cut each artichoke in half vertically and serve with reduced-calorie mayonnaise.

Calories per serving: 33
Calcium per serving: 26mg

BEVERAGES

Tropical Teaser

Serves 3

240ml (8 fl oz) pineapple juice
120 ml (4 fl oz) evaporated skimmed milk
5 tablespoons skimmed milk powder
$\frac{1}{4}$ teaspoon coconut essence, or to taste
$\frac{1}{4}$ teaspoon rum essence, or to taste
1 ripe medium-sized banana, sliced
6 ice cubes

1. Pour the pineapple juice and evaporated milk into a blender container; add the skimmed milk powder and blend until smooth. Add the essences and banana and blend again until smooth.
2. Add the ice cubes one at a time and blend on low speed after each addition. Increase speed to high and blend until thick and frothy, about 30 seconds.

Calories per serving: 129
Calcium per serving: 220mg

Berry Delight

Serves 2

240ml (8 fl oz) natural yogurt
2 tablespoons raspberry jam
240ml (8 fl oz) water
100g ($3\frac{1}{2}$oz) frozen unsweetened
  raspberries

1. Pour the yogurt, jam and water in a blender container and blend together.
2. Add the berries slowly and blend until smooth.

Calories per serving: 151
Calcium per serving: 225mg

Mocha Instant Breakfast

With just enough caffeine to get you going in the morning!

Serves 2

180ml (6 fl oz) whole milk, very cold
100g (3½ oz) skimmed milk powder
½ teaspoon instant coffee
2 teaspoons cocoa powder
1 tablespoon sugar
pinch of salt
5 ice cubes

1. Place milk and skimmed milk powder in a blender container. Add the coffee, cocoa powder, sugar and salt and blend until smooth.
2. Add the ice cubes one at a time, blending at low speed after each addition. Increase speed to high and blend until thick and frothy, about 30 seconds.

Calories per serving: 163
Calcium per serving: 391 mg

Old-Fashioned Hot Cocoa

Serves 6

75g (2½ oz) sugar
40g (1½ oz) cocoa powder
¼ teaspoon salt
360ml (12 fl oz) water
1 litre (1¾ pints) whole milk
160g (5¾ oz) skimmed milk powder
½ teaspoon peppermint essence (optional)

1. Mix the sugar, cocoa powder and salt in a 2-litre (3½ pint) saucepan. Add the water and bring to the boil, stirring constantly. Boil and stir for 2 minutes. Add milk, then slowly add skimmed milk powder, stirring constantly. Heat thoroughly, but do not boil. Stir in peppermint essence if desired.
2. Just before serving, whisk with an electric whisk until foamy.

Calories per serving: 202
Calcium per serving: 365mg

Banana Tofu Shake

Tofu, a versatile protein and calcium source, is the basis for this quick breakfast drink.

Serves 6

750ml (1¼ pints) orange juice
390g (14 oz) soft tofu
2 ripe bananas, sliced

1. Pour orange juice into a blender container. Add tofu and bananas and blend until smooth.

Calories per serving: 140
Calcium per serving: 97mg

SOUPS

Boston-Style Clam Chowder

Serves 6

360ml (12 fl oz) chicken or vegetable stock
195g (7 oz) diced cauliflower
150g (5½ oz) peeled and diced potatoes
170g (6 oz) onions, chopped
70g (2½ oz) fresh mushrooms, sliced
1 teaspoon dried dillweed
¼ teaspoon dried marjoram
¼ teaspoon salt
pinch of freshly ground black pepper
240ml (8 fl oz) evaporated skimmed milk
280g (10 oz) tinned clams, drained
chopped parsley to garnish

1. Heat stock to boiling in a large saucepan and add cauliflower. Cover and simmer 10-12 minutes. Remove cauliflower with a slotted spoon and set aside to cool.
2. Add potatoes, onions, mushrooms, dillweed, marjoram, salt and pepper to stock and return to the boil. Cover and simmer 15 minutes, stirring occasionally.
3. Meanwhile, place cauliflower and milk in a blender container and blend until smooth. After the soup has simmered for 15 minutes, add the puréed cauliflower, stirring over low heat until thick. Add the clams. Increase the heat to moderate and bring to the boil. Boil for 1 minute.
4. Pour into soup bowls and garnish with parsley.

Calories per serving: 103
Calcium per serving: 167mg

Cream of Broccoli Soup

Serves 5

480ml (16 fl oz) chicken or vegetable stock
280g (10 oz) frozen broccoli, chopped
4 tablespoons chopped parsley
1 medium-sized onion, chopped
2 tablespoons lemon juice
480ml (16 fl oz) evaporated skimmed milk
1 tablespoon cornflour
dash of freshly grated nutmeg
2 teaspoons garlic salt
pinch of freshly ground black pepper
chopped parsley to garnish

1. Heat the stock to boiling in a large saucepan with the broccoli, chopped parsley, onion and lemon juice. Cover and simmer until the broccoli is tender, according to packet instructions. Remove vegetables from the stock with a slotted spoon and set aside to cool.
2. Place the vegetables in a blender container and add evaporated milk until the blender is three-quarters full. Add the cornflour and blend until smooth.
3. Slowly stir the puréed vegetables, the remainder of the evaporated milk and the nutmeg, garlic salt and pepper into the stock. Heat over a low heat until thickened, stirring constantly. Bring to the boil and boil lightly for 1 minute.
4. Serve hot, garnished with parsley.

Calories per serving: 125
Calcium per serving: 355mg

Cream of Mushroom Soup

It's actually milk, not cream, that makes this soup light, lively and rich in calcium.

Serves 6

225g (8 oz) fresh mushrooms
170g (6 oz) onions, chopped
30g (1 oz) margarine
1 teaspoon salt (omit if stock is salty)
pinch of ground white pepper
480ml (16 fl oz) chicken or
   vegetable stock
3 tablespoons cornflour
360ml (12 fl oz) evaporated skimmed milk
chopped parsley to garnish

1. Slice enough mushrooms into a measuring jug to measure 240g (8 oz) in volume; chop the remainder.
2. Stir-fry the sliced mushrooms in a nonstick frying pan over a low heat until golden. Set aside.
3. In a medium-sized saucepan, melt the margarine and cook the chopped mushrooms and onions until tender. Stir in the salt, if using and the pepper. Cook, stirring over low heat for approximately 1 minute. Remove from the heat.
4. Pour the stock into the mushroom-onion mixture and bring to the boil, stirring occasionally. Blend the cornflour into the milk until smooth and then add to the saucepan with the sliced mushrooms. Bring to the boil and boil lightly for 1 minute.
5. Serve hot, garnished with parsley.

Calories per serving: 127
Calcium per serving: 198mg

Cream of Spinach Soup

A thick, spicy soup packed with nutrition.

Serves 6

280g (10 oz) frozen chopped spinach or
   fresh spinach, cooked
85g (3 oz) skimmed milk powder
$1\frac{1}{4}$ pints skimmed milk
2 tablespoons chopped onion
1 tablespoon cornflour
1 teaspoon salt
$\frac{1}{2}$ teaspoon freshly ground black pepper
$\frac{1}{4}$-$\frac{1}{2}$ teaspoon curry powder

1. Cook frozen spinach, if using, according
   to packet directions. Drain and allow to
   cool.
2. In a blender container, blend skimmed
   milk powder and liquid milk until smooth
   and free of lumps. Pour into a jug and set
   aside.
3. In a food processor or blender, process the
   spinach and onion until smooth (the
   mixture does not have to be completely
   puréed).
4. Add the cornflour to a small quantity of
   the milk mixture in a small screw-topped
   jar. Cover and shake to blend.
5. In a large saucepan, combine the
   cornflour mixture, milk mixture and
   spinach mixture. Add the salt, pepper and
   curry powder and heat over a low heat
   until thickened, stirring constantly.
   Increase the heat and heat to boiling.
6. Serve immediately.

Calories per serving: 91
Calcium per serving: 312mg

Creamy Rice Soup

A delicious change-of-pace soup.

Serves 8

100g (3½ oz) cauliflower, diced
480ml (16 fl oz) chicken or beef stock
100g (3½ oz) skimmed milk powder
280g (10 oz) cooked rice
1 teaspoon salt
3 spring onions, sliced diagonally
2 egg yolks, well-beaten

1. In a large saucepan cook cauliflower in stock until tender, 10-12 minutes. Remove from stock with a slotted spoon and cool slightly.
2. Place cooked cauliflower, milk and skimmed milk powder in a blender container and blend until smooth.
3. Add milk mixture, rice, salt and spring onions to stock and heat over a low heat, stirring constantly until hot and of the desired consistency.
4. Just before serving, stir in the beaten egg yolks, passing them through a fine sieve into the hot soup.

Calories per serving: 117
Calcium per serving: 176mg

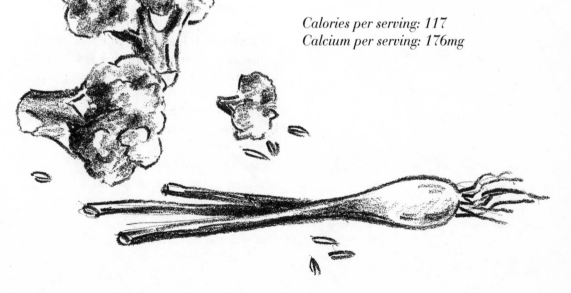

Hearty Bean Soup

Serve with a green salad and Cornbread (page 122) or scones.

450g (1 lb) dried haricot beans, washed and
  drained
3 litres (5 pints) water
2 knuckles of bacon
300ml (10¾oz) beef consommé
2 cloves garlic, finely chopped
1 bay leaf
½ teaspoon salt
½ teaspoon freshly ground black pepper
420g (15 oz) cooked, mashed potatoes
3 medium-sized onions, chopped
170g (6 oz) celery, diced (including leaves)
4 tablespoons finely chopped parsley
225g (8 oz) carrots, diced
2 tablespoons cider vinegar

1. Cover dry beans with water in a stock pot; bring to the boil and boil 2 minutes. Remove from the heat, cover and allow to stand for 1 hour.
2. Add knuckles of bacon, consommé, garlic, bay leaf, salt and pepper to the beans and simmer, covered, for 2 hours.
3. Remove the knuckles of bacon with a slotted spoon; cut off the fat and bone and cut the bacon into cubes and set aside.
4. Add enough soup liquid to the mashed potatoes to make them soft and runny; mix well, then add the potatoes to the stock pot with the onions, celery, parsley, carrots and bacon. Cover and simmer for a further 1-1½ hours. Stir in the cider vinegar and simmer a further few minutes.

Calories per serving: 200
Calcium per serving: 78mg

Marvellous Meatless Chilli

Great for leftovers, this low-calorie chilli is one of Judy's favourites.

Serves 16

170g (6 oz) carrots, sliced
170g (6 oz) onions, chopped
170g (6 oz) green peppers, chopped
170g (6 oz) celery, sliced
420g (15 oz) tinned tomatoes
420g (15 oz) tomato sauce
170g (6 oz) tomato purée
180ml (6 fl oz) tomato juice
juice of 1 lemon
840g (30 oz) tinned kidney beans, drained
    (reserve liquid)
840g (30 oz) tinned chick peas, drained
3 cloves garlic, finely chopped
2-3 tablespoons chilli powder
1 teaspoon sugar
$\frac{1}{2}$ tablespoon dried basil
1 teaspoon salt
$\frac{1}{2}$ teaspoon freshly ground black pepper
$\frac{1}{2}$ teaspoon hot pepper sauce

1. Place the carrots, onions, peppers and celery in a large nonstick saucepan and cook until just barely tender, stirring occasionally.
2. Add the rest of the ingredients and mix well. If the mixture is too thick, add the reserved kidney bean liquid. Cover and simmer for about 20 minutes. Do not overcook or the vegetables will be mushy.

Calories per serving: 122
Calcium per serving: 48mg

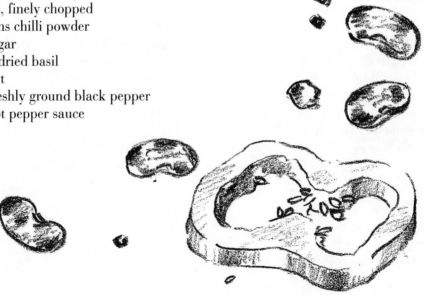

Green Soup

Serves 10

1 small bunch brightly coloured greens
   (spring greens, Swiss chard, sorrel, kale)
1.8 litres ($3\frac{1}{4}$ pints) chicken or vegetable
   stock
1 tablespoon fish sauce
$\frac{1}{2}$ tablespoon sugar
2 spring onions, chopped
3-4 thin slices root ginger

1. Remove root ends and imperfect leaves
   from the greens. Wash thoroughly and
   drain.
2. Heat the stock; add all the ingredients
   except the greens and simmer for 10
   minutes. Add the greens and simmer for a
   further 3 minutes. Serve hot.

Calories per serving: 39
Calcium per serving: 34mg

Tofu Chicken Soup

Serves 8

900ml ($1\frac{1}{2}$ pints) chicken stock
225g (8 oz) Chinese cabbage, chopped
2 stalks celery, chopped
70g ($2\frac{1}{2}$ oz) fresh mushrooms, sliced
310g (11 oz) tofu, cubed
140g (5 oz) cooked chicken breast, shredded
few drops sesame oil
2 spring onions, finely chopped

1. Bring the stock to the boil in a large
   saucepan. Add the cabbage; cover and
   simmer for 1 hour.
2. Add the celery and simmer for 10
   minutes. Add the mushrooms, tofu,
   chicken and sesame oil and simmer for a
   further 5-10 minutes.
3. To serve, pour into bowls and garnish
   with spring onion.

Calories per serving: 86
Calcium per serving: 73mg

Watercress Soup

A light beginning to a Chinese dinner.

Serves 5

1 bunch watercress, washed and cut into
  thirds
900ml (1½ pints) chicken stock
1 thin slice root ginger
2 spring onions, thinly sliced

1. Combine watercress, stock and ginger in
a 2-litre (3½ pint) saucepan. Simmer for
15-20 minutes (or longer, if desired).
Purée in a blender. Garnish each serving
with spring onion.

Calories per serving: 34
Calcium per serving: 46mg

SALADS

Garlic Salad à la Rena

Serves 4

225g (8 oz) cos lettuce
2 large tomatoes, sliced
2 spring onions, chopped
35g (1¼ oz) fresh mushrooms, sliced
110g (4 oz) feta cheese, crumbled
30g (1 oz) black olives, stoned and sliced
   (optional)

Dressing:
1 large clove garlic
¼ - ½ teaspoon salt
1 teaspoon olive oil
juice of ½ large lemon

1. First make the dressing: chop the garlic into small pieces. Mash together with the salt. Add olive oil, then lemon juice, blending after each addition.
2. Toss the lettuce, tomatoes, spring onions and mushrooms together in a large bowl. Add the dressing and toss again. Top with the feta cheese and black olives, if using. Serve immediately.

Calories per serving: 130
Calcium per serving: 267mg

65

Refreshing Fruit Salad

This unique fruit salad is sure to get rave reviews!

Serves 6

225g (8 oz) low fat soft cheese, at room
   temperature
240ml (8 fl oz) cherry (or other fruit
   flavour) yogurt
1 tablespoon sugar
dash of vanilla essence
$\frac{1}{4}$ teaspoon salt
450g (16 oz) tinned stoned dark sweet
   cherries, drained
1 medium orange, cut into segments, then
   halved
225g (8 oz) tinned crushed pineapple
   (packed in juice), drained
70g ($2\frac{1}{2}$ oz) dried currants
salad greens

1. Beat the cheese in a large mixing bowl
   with an electric mixer until smooth. Using
   a low speed, beat in the yogurt, sugar,
   vanilla essence and salt.
2. Set aside 6-12 cherries for decoration.
   Stir the remaining cherries, orange,
   pineapple and currants into the cheese
   mixture. Pour into a 1-litre ($1\frac{3}{4}$ pint)
   mould or 6 individual moulds and freeze
   for at least 8 hours.
3. Remove mould(s) from freezer and let
   stand until softened (about 45-60
   minutes for a large mould). Unmould on
   salad greens and decorate with reserved
   cherries.

Calories per serving: 265
Calcium per serving: 115mg

Almond-Carrot Salad

Serves 4

3-4 medium-sized carrots, finely shredded
3 dried figs, chopped
30g (1 oz) chopped almonds
¼ teaspoon salt
120ml (4 fl oz) Cooked Salad Dressing (see
  page 112)

1. Mix all the ingredients together in a salad
   bowl. Cover and refrigerate for at least 1
   hour before serving.

Calories per serving: 152
Calcium per serving: 102mg

Blackberry-Almond Mould

Serves 5

225g (8 oz) tinned blackberries (reserve
  juice)
1 packet blackberry or cherry jelly
240ml (8 fl oz) vanilla-flavoured yogurt
1¼ oz blanched chopped almonds
salad greens

1. Drain the blackberries, reserving the
   juice. Set the blackberries aside.
2. Make up the jelly according to the packet
   directions using the reserved blackberry
   juice as part of the liquid. Cool.
3. Add the yogurt to the jelly and whip until
   smooth. Refrigerate until slightly
   thickened, but not set.
3. Stir the berries and almonds into the jelly
   mixture and pour into a 1-litre ring
   mould or 5 individual moulds. Refrigerate
   until firm.
4. Serve on salad greens.

Calories per serving: 202
Calcium per serving: 98mg

Caesar Salad

Serve with Prawn and Cheese Soufflé (page 90) and French bread.

Serves 6

1 egg
1 tablespoon olive oil
$\frac{1}{4}$ teaspoon garlic powder
55g (2 oz) white bread, crusts removed and
  cubed
1 clove garlic, crushed
$\frac{1}{4}$ teaspoon mustard powder
$\frac{1}{2}$ teaspoon salt
$\frac{1}{4}$ teaspoon freshly ground black pepper
2 tablespoons olive oil
2 tablespoons water
$\frac{1}{2}$ tablespoon Worcestershire sauce
8 anchovy fillets, drained and chopped
1 large bunch cos lettuce, torn
30g (1 oz) grated parmesan cheese
30g(1 oz) blue cheese, crumbled
2 tablespoons lemon juice

1. Warm the cold egg by immersing in tepid water. In a small saucepan, boil enough water to cover the egg completely. Lower the egg into the boiling water with a spoon. Remove from the heat and allow to stand for 30 seconds. Immediately cool egg under a running tap to prevent further cooking.
2. Heat 1 tablespoon olive oil and the garlic powder in a nonstick frying pan. Add the bread cubes and sauté until golden-brown, stirring often. Remove from the heat.
3. Make the dressing: combine the garlic, mustard powder, salt, pepper, oil, water, Worcestershire sauce and anchovies in a screw-topped jar; cover and shake vigorously.
4. Put the lettuce into a large salad bowl. Pour the dressing over, add the cheeses and toss until the lettuce is well-coated. Break the egg into the centre of the salad. Pour the lemon juice on top of the egg and toss well. Add the bread cubes, toss gently and serve immediately.

Calories per serving: 136
Calcium per serving: 143mg

Double Bean Salad

If you don't like traditional bean salads, try this one! The combination of spices makes it very unusual.

Serves 8

170g (10 oz) home-cooked or tinned chick peas, drained
170g (10 oz) home-cooked or tinned kidney beans, drained
85g (3 oz) celery, diced
1 tablespoon finely chopped fresh coriander
2 tablespoons finely chopped fresh parsley
180ml (6 fl oz) Spicy Yogurt Dressing (page 114)

1. Combine all ingredients in a salad bowl. Refrigerate before serving.

Calories per serving: 118
Calcium per serving: 97mg

Salmon-Macaroni Salad

This salad is a complete meal and can be served either as a main course dish or side dish.

Serves 18 as a side dish, 6 as a main course

335g (12 oz) short-cut macaroni
439g (15½ oz) tinned salmon
250g (9 oz) sweetcorn, cooked
250g (9 oz) red and/or green peppers,
    chopped
85g (3 oz) onion, chopped
110g (4 oz) celery, chopped
salt and freshly ground black pepper
140ml (5 fl oz) reduced-calorie mayonnaise
140ml (5 fl oz) natural yogurt
paprika
raw spinach leaves to serve

1. Cook the macaroni according to the packet directions, omitting salt. Drain and allow to cool.
2. Drain the salmon and break into chunks in a large bowl. Add the macaroni, sweetcorn, peppers, onion, celery and salt and pepper to taste, mixing well.
3. Blend together the mayonnaise and yogurt and fold into the salad.
4. To serve, line salad plates with spinach leaves, mound the salad on top and sprinkle with paprika.

Calories per serving: 152 as a side dish; 456 as a main course
Calcium per serving: 74mg as a side dish; 222mg as a main course

Salmon–Tofu Salad

A family favourite.

Serves 6

390g (14 oz) firm tofu
2 large tomatoes, cubed
195g (7 oz) tinned salmon
3 spring onions, chopped
1 tablespoon sesame seeds

Sesame Dressing:
4 tablespoons soy sauce
2 tablespoons rice vinegar
2 teaspoons sesame oil
2 tablespoons white wine

1. First make the dressing. Pour ingredients into a screw-topped jar and shake vigorously.
2. Drain the tofu and cut into cubes. Place in a salad bowl.
3. Arrange the tomatoes over the tofu, then shred salmon over. Sprinkle with spring onions and sesame seeds. Just before serving, pour the dressing over.

Calories per serving: 135
Calcium per serving: 168mg

Spinach Salad

Serves 8

2 tablespoons sesame seeds
450g (1 lb) fresh spinach
85g (3 oz) cheddar cheese, grated
2 spring onions, sliced
420g (15 oz) tinned unsweetened pineapple
   chunks, drained (reserve juice)
3 hard-boiled eggs, sliced
70g (2½ oz) fresh mushrooms, sliced

Dressing:
1 tablespoon oil
4 tablespoons pineapple juice (reserved from
   the tinned fruit)
2 tablespoons white wine vinegar
½ teaspoon garlic salt
½ teaspoon ground ginger

1. Toast sesame seeds in a nonstick frying
   pan. Set aside.
2. Combine the dressing ingredients in a
   screw-topped jar. Shake well to blend;
   refrigerate for several hours.
3. Remove root ends, coarse stalks and
   imperfect leaves from spinach. Wash
   spinach thoroughly, drain well, dry with
   absorbent kitchen paper and tear into
   chunks in a large salad bowl.
4. Add the cheese, spring onions and
   pineapple to the spinach and toss well.
   Garnish with the eggs and mushrooms.
5. Just before serving, remove the dressing
   from the refrigerator, shake well, pour
   over the salad and toss lightly. Sprinkle
   the reserved sesame seeds on top.

Calories per serving: 143
Calcium per serving: 143mg

Zesty Broccoli Salad

Serves 4

560g (1¼ lb) frozen broccoli florets
55g (2 oz) mature cheddar cheese, grated
4 tablespoons imitation bacon bits, optional
3 tablespoons reduced-calorie mayonnaise

1. Thaw the broccoli thoroughly. Drain off excess liquid and chop into a salad bowl. Combine with cheese and bacon bits, if using. Toss with mayonnaise.
2. Cover and chill in the refrigerator before serving.

Calories per serving: 140
Calcium per serving: 179mg

MAIN COURSE DISHES

Ann's Special Spinach Pie _____

This crustless pie is very easy to make—and great for leftovers.

Serves 6

225g (8 oz) mature cheddar cheese,
   grated
5 tablespoons wholemeal flour
$\frac{1}{4}$ teaspoon salt
$\frac{1}{2}$ teaspoon freshly ground black pepper
1 teaspoon garlic powder
4 eggs
450g (1 lb) low fat cottage cheese
85g (3 oz) onion, chopped
280g (10 oz) frozen chopped spinach,
   thawed and drained well
paprika

1. Preheat the oven to 350°F (180°C/Gas Mark 4).
2. Blend the cheddar cheese, flour, salt, pepper and garlic powder together in a mixing bowl.
3. In another large bowl, beat the eggs and cottage cheese with an electric whisk for about 2 minutes. Add the cheddar cheese mixture, onion and spinach; blend thoroughly.
4. Pour into a greased 22.5cm (9-inch) glass pie tin. Sprinkle with paprika. Bake for 1 hour.

Calories per serving: 310
Calcium per serving: 407mg

Baked Soya Beans

If you've never cooked with soya beans before, this is a great starter recipe: easy and delicious! Serve with a hearty bread and a salad for a complete meal.

Serves 4

280g (10 oz) dried soya beans, washed and
   picked over
900ml (1½ pints) water (for soaking)
225g (8 oz) tomato sauce
1 large onion, chopped
2 tablespoons molasses
2 teaspoons oil
3 tablespoons firmly packed muscovado
   sugar
¼ teaspoon mustard powder
pinch of freshly ground black pepper
2 tablespoons imitation bacon bits
   (optional)

1. Soak beans overnight in the measured water in a large saucepan, or boil the beans in the water for 2 minutes, remove from the heat, skim off loose bean skins and allowed to stand, covered for 1 hour.
2. Pour out the soaking water and cover the beans with fresh water. Bring to the boil over a moderate heat, then reduce the heat, cover and simmer until the beans are soft and tender, not crunchy, at least 2 hours. Drain.
3. Place beans in a mixing bowl and mix in remaining ingredients. Transfer to a 1.5 litre (2½ pint) casserole. Cover and bake at 350°F (180°C/Gas Mark 4) for 3-5 hours, stirring occasionally. Add extra water if the beans become too dry.

Calories per serving: 360
Calcium per serving: 216mg

Broccoli-Stuffed Pasta

Serves 6

170g (6 oz) jumbo pasta shells
450g (1 lb) frozen chopped broccoli, thawed
450g (1 lb) low fat cottage cheese
225g (8 oz) mozzarella cheese, grated
55g (2 oz) grated parmesan cheese
1 tablespoon grated onion
$\frac{1}{2}$ teaspoon freshly ground black pepper
2 cloves crushed garlic
870g ($1\frac{1}{2}$ pints) marinara or spaghetti sauce

1. Cook pasta according to packet directions. Drain and set aside.
2. Combine the broccoli, cottage cheese, 170g (6 oz) of the mozzarella cheese, parmesan cheese, onion, pepper and garlic in a large bowl.
3. Spoon enough sauce into a large ovenproof dish to cover the base. Fill the shells with the broccoli mixture and arrange over the sauce in a single layer. Spoon the remaining sauce on top and sprinkle with the remaining mozzarella cheese.
4. Preheat the oven to 375°F (190°C/Gas Mark 5). Bake the pasta until heated through, about 30 minutes, covering the dish with aluminium foil during the first 15 minutes. Serve hot.

Calories per serving: 437
Calcium per serving: 493mg

Charlene's Spicy Pork Tofu

Serves 4

110g (4 oz) courgettes
390g (14 oz) firm tofu
110g (4 oz) minced pork
1 teaspoon finely chopped garlic
1 teaspoon finely chopped root ginger
420ml (14 fl oz) chicken stock
2 tablespoons cornflour
2 tablespoons soy sauce
$1\frac{1}{2}$ tablespoons sugar
$\frac{1}{2}$ tablespoon chilli sauce
2 tablespoons chopped spring onion

1. Cut courgettes and tofu into 1.25cm ($\frac{1}{2}$-inch) cubes.
2. Brown the pork in a nonstick frying pan. Add the garlic, ginger and courgettes; cover and simmer until the courgettes are tender. Remove from the heat.
3. Combine the stock, cornflour, soy sauce, sugar and chilli sauce in a small bowl.
4. Return the pork mixture to the hob, increase the heat to medium-high and add the stock mixture, stirring until the sauce thickens. Boil and stir for 1 minute. Gently fold in the tofu and spring onion. Heat thoroughly and serve immediately.

Calories per serving: 205
Calcium per serving: 140mg

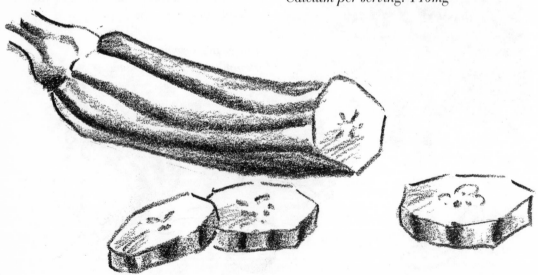

Cheesy Aubergine Parmesan

Serves 6

1 large aubergine
780g (28 oz) tomato sauce
2 teaspoons dried basil, crumbled
1 teaspoon dried thyme, crumbled
3 tablespoons finely chopped parsley
$\frac{1}{2}$ tablespoon garlic powder
$\frac{1}{4}$ teaspoon salt
pinch of freshly ground black pepper
225g (8 oz) low fat cottage cheese, drained
  well
110g (4 oz) mozzarella cheese, grated
110g (4 oz) mild cheddar cheese, grated
30 g (1 oz) grated parmesan cheese
1 tablespoon plain flour

1. Slice the aubergine crossways into
   1.25cm ($\frac{1}{2}$-inch) slices. Steam for 10
   minutes, remove from the heat and set
   aside.
2. Meanwhile, in a medium-sized saucepan,
   simmer the tomato sauce, basil and
   thyme to reduce.
3. In a bowl, mix together the parsley, garlic
   powder, salt, pepper, cottage cheese,
   mozzarella cheese, half the parmesan
   cheese and the flour.
4. Preheat the oven to 350°F (180°C/Gas
   Mark 4).
5. Place half the steamed aubergine in the
   bottom of a shallow 2-litre ($3\frac{1}{2}$ pint)
   casserole. Add half of the cheese mixture
   and half of the remaining tomato sauce.
   Repeat the layers and top with the
   remaining parmesan cheese.
6. Bake, uncovered for 30 minutes.

Calories per serving: 263
Calcium per serving: 383mg

Chicken á la Queen

This calcium-packed version of a traditional dish is fit for a queen.

Serves 6

14 oz (115 g) can mushroom stems and
   pieces, drained (reserve liquid)
1 small green pepper, chopped
3 tablespoons margarine
3 tablespoons cornflour
$\frac{1}{2}$ teaspoon salt
$\frac{1}{4}$ teaspoon pepper
$\frac{1}{2}$ teaspoon ground marjoram
1 chicken stock cube
1 pint skimmed milk
12 oz (340g) chicken, skinless, cooked and
   cut-up
14 oz (115 g) jar whole pimientos, chopped
2 lb (900g) potatoes, mashed as Creamy
   Mashed Potatoes, p96

1. In a medium saucepan, cook and stir mushrooms and green pepper in margarine over medium heat for 5 minutes.
2. Remove from heat and sprinkle in cornflour, salt, pepper and marjoram.
3. Cook over low heat, stirring constantly, just until smooth; remove from heat.
4. Stir in bouillon cube, milk and reserved mushroom liquid until smooth. Heat to boiling, stirring constantly. Boil and stir 1 minute.
5. Stir in chicken and pimientos; heat thoroughly. Serve over mashed potatoes.

Calories per serving: 347
Calcium per serving: 242

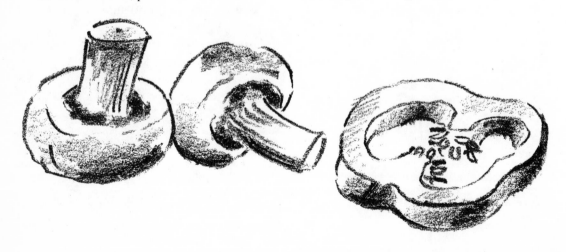

Chicken Enchiladas

Even the strictest waist-watcher will enjoy this low fat version of a favourite Mexican dish.

Serves 6

1½ chicken breasts, skinned
420ml (14 fl oz) homemade chicken stock,
    fat skimmed off
4 tablespoons cornflour
780g (28 oz) enchilada sauce
1 teaspoon sugar
1 teaspoon chilli powder
12 tortillas
480ml (16 fl oz) natural yogurt
55g (2 oz) mozzarella cheese, grated
55g (2 oz) reduced-fat cheddar cheese or
    processed cheese, diced
1 large onion, finely chopped
85g (3 oz) mature cheddar cheese, grated
85g (3 oz) mild cheddar cheese, grated
2 spring onions, chopped

1. Cook the chicken in water to cover until tender. Cool, then shred the meat finely, discarding the bones. Reserve 420ml (14 fl oz) of the cooking stock.
2. Dissolve the cornflour completely in 110g (4 oz) of the enchilada sauce. Pour the remaining sauce into a saucepan, blend in the cornflour mixture, sugar and chilli powder.
3. Soften the tortillas by wrapping them in stacks of 6 in moistened absorbent kitchen paper and then in foil. Seal the foil tightly and heat in a 250°F (120°C/Gas Mark ½) oven for 15 minutes.
4. Meanwhile, whisk the yogurt with a fork until smooth; add a small amount of the reserved stock to thin, then add the yogurt and the remaining stock to the enchilada sauce mixture. Stir over a medium-low heat, adding the mozzarella and processed cheddar cheese. Continue cooking until the cheeses are melted. Do not boil.
5. To assemble the enchiladas, unwrap the warmed tortillas. Fill each with a portion of the chicken, onion, some of the mature cheddar and 1 tablespoon sauce. Roll up and place, seam side down in a large baking dish. Top with the sauce. Sprinkle with the remaining mature cheddar and the mild cheddar.
6. Increase the oven temperature to 350°F (180°C/Gas Mark 4) and bake the enchiladas until the cheese is melted and the sauce is bubbly, about 25-30 minutes. Garnish with spring onions.

Calories per serving: 458
Calcium per serving: 617mg

Falafel Sandwiches with Tahini Sauce

A Middle Eastern delight!

Serves 8

195g (7 oz) dried chick peas
1.1 litres (2 pints) water for soaking
2 cloves garlic, finely chopped
½ teaspoon salt
85g (3 oz) onion, very finely chopped
2 tablespoons very finely chopped parsley
1 tablespoon very finely chopped fresh
  coriander
1 teaspoon ground cumin
1 tablespoon lemon juice
pinch of freshly ground black pepper
pinch of cayenne pepper
1 teaspoon olive oil
1 teaspoon bicarbonate of soda
8 pitta breads
4 tomatoes, sliced
225g (8 oz) mature cheddar cheese, grated
140g (5 oz) iceberg lettuce, shredded
Tahini Dipping Sauce (page 115)

1. Soak chick peas in the measured water
   overnight. Drain.
2. Rinse the beans and place in a saucepan
   with water to cover. Bring to the boil,
   then simmer about 35-45 minutes, or
   until tender. Remove from the heat and
   drain again.
3. Meanwhile, crush the garlic with the salt,
   then mix in onion, parsley, coriander,
   cumin, lemon juice, black and cayenne
   peppers and oil.
4. Place the chick peas and bicarbonate of
   soda in a food processor or blender and
   process until the mixture resembles coarse
   breadcrumbs. (Do not process to a paste.)
5. Combine the chick peas with the
   seasoning mixture and form into 20-22
   patties 4.5cm (1¾ inches) in diameter,
   approximately 2cm (¾-jnch) thick in the
   middle and less thick at the edges.
6. Preheat the oven to 350°F (180°C/Gas
   Mark 4).
7. Place the chick pea patties on a baking
   sheet and bake for 15 minutes. Remove
   from the oven.
8. To assemble the sandwiches, put 2 or 3
   patties into each pitta bread. Add tomato
   slices, shredded cheese and lettuce and
   top with 2 tablespoons Tahini Dipping
   Sauce.

Calories per serving: 349
Calcium per serving: 283mg

Garden Burrito

Serves 1

1 20cm (8-inch) flour tortilla
85g (3 oz) tinned drained pinto beans
70g (2½ oz) lettuce, shredded
1 tomato, chopped
1 tablespoon chopped onion
55g (2 oz) cheddar cheese, grated
salsa to taste

1. Wrap the tortilla in damp absorbent kitchen paper and then in foil and warm in a low oven or microwave oven to soften.
2. Mash the beans with a fork and cook over a moderate heat, stirring occasionally.
3. Spread the beans on the warmed tortilla. Top with the lettuce, tomato, onion, cheese and salsa.

Calories per serving: 527
Calcium per serving: 551mg

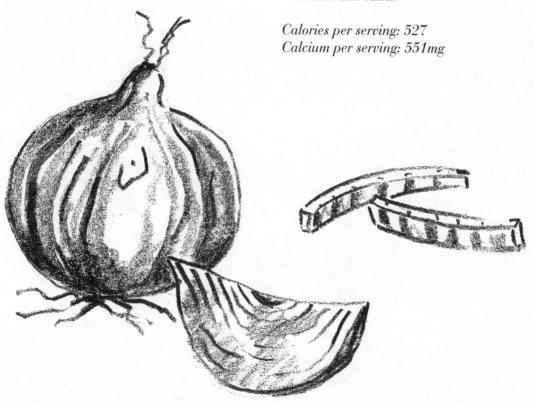

Italian Pasta Salad

This is a meal in itself.

Serves 14

450g (1 lb) small pasta shells
110g (4 oz) each: ham, salami and
    pepperoni, cut up
225g (8 oz) mozzarella cheese, cut up
225g (8 oz) cheddar cheese, cut up
3 green peppers, diced
4 tomatoes, diced
3 spring onions, diced
4 stalks celery, diced
85g (3 oz) black olives, stoned and sliced

Dressing:
120ml (4 fl oz) vegetable oil
120ml (4 fl oz) white vinegar
60ml (2 fl oz) dry white wine
$\frac{1}{2}$ teaspoon dried oregano
2 cloves garlic, crushed

1. Cook pasta shells according to the packet directions. Rinse with cold running water and cool.
2. Meanwhile, make the dressing. Place all the ingredients in a screw-topped jar and shake vigorously.
3. When the pasta is cool, mix with the other salad ingredients, pour the dressing over and toss well.

Calories per serving: 398
Calcium per serving: 259mg

Mexican Quiche

The crust used in this quiche is lower in fat and calories than ordinary pie crust.

Serves 6

125g (4½ oz) scone baking mix or
   110g (4 oz) plain flour
2 teaspoons baking powder
2 teaspoons sugar
½ teaspoon salt
½ teaspoon cream of tartar
110g (4 oz) solid vegetable fat
4 tablespoons + 1 teaspoon cold water
240ml (8 fl oz) evaporated skimmed milk
3 eggs, slightly beaten
pinch of ground cumin
85g (3 oz) mozzarella cheese, grated
55g (2 oz) mild cheddar cheese, grated
140g (5 oz) mature cheddar cheese, grated
110g (4 oz) tinned green chillies, drained
   and chopped

1. Preheat the oven to 425°F (220°C/Gas Mark 7).
2. Mix the baking mix with the cold water until a dough forms, or, if you are starting from scratch, sift the flour, baking powder, sugar, salt and cream of tartar together, then cut the fat in with a knife until the mixture resembles coarse breadcrumbs, then add the water. On a floured board, knead the dough about 10 times, then roll out or pat into a 22.5cm (9-inch) pie tin. Bake for 10 minutes, or until it is pale golden in colour. Remove from the oven.
3. Whisk the milk, eggs and cumin together until blended.
4. Reduce the oven temperature to 325°F (160°C/Gas Mark 3).
5. Sprinkle the mozzarella, mild cheddar and half the mature cheddar cheese over the partially-baked crust. Distribute the chillies over the cheese, then pour over the milk mixture. Sprinkle with the remaining cheese.
5. Bake the quiche for 55-60 minutes or until the centre is set (shake gently to test). Allow to stand for 15 minutes before cutting into wedges.

Calories per serving: 329
Calcium per serving: 476mg

Michigan Meatloaf

Serves 10

900g (2 lb) best beef mince
2 eggs, beaten
160g (5½ oz) skimmed milk powder
1 medium-sized onion, diced
55g (2 oz) dry breadcrumbs
1 teaspoon dried Italian seasoning
2 teaspoons salt
½ teaspoon garlic powder

1. Preheat the oven to 350°F (180°C/Gas Mark 4).
2. Mix all ingredients well; pack into a 1-litre (2-lb) loaf pan or pat into a loaf and place in a baking tin.
3. Bake, covered for about 1½ hours.

Calories per serving: 212
Calcium per serving: 106mg

Oriental Omelette

Serves 3

280g (10 oz) firm tofu, drained and finely cubed
3 eggs, lightly beaten
1 tablespoon soy sauce
¼ teaspoon honey
1 tablespoon sesame oil
3 large fresh mushrooms, sliced
2 spring onions, chopped

1. Combine the tofu, eggs, soy sauce and honey in a large bowl and mix well.
2. Heat the oil in a large nonstick frying pan. Add the mushrooms and spring onions and sauté 2-3 minutes, until slightly cooked. Add the contents of the frying pan to the tofu-egg mixture and stir. Pour back into the frying pan and cook over a low heat, lifting the edges gently to allow the uncooked egg to flow underneath. When the omelette is cooked, fold and serve immediately.

Calories per serving: 193
Calcium per serving: 149mg

Oysters Parmesan

Serves 4

1 tablespoon olive oil
1 large onion, chopped
$\frac{1}{2}$ teaspoon dried thyme
$\frac{1}{4}$ teaspoon dried oregano
3 cloves garlic, finely chopped
3 tablespoons chopped parsley
$\frac{1}{4}$ teaspoon Tabasco
salt and freshly ground black pepper
450g (1 lb) shelled oysters with liquor
110 g (4 oz) dry breadcrumbs, mixed with 1
  teaspoon dried Italian seasoning
70g (2$\frac{1}{2}$ oz) grated parmesan cheese

1. Heat the oil in a nonstick frying pan. Add
   the onion and sauté until soft, but not
   coloured. Add the thyme, oregano, garlic,
   parsley, Tabasco and salt and pepper to
   taste. Mix well.
2. Preheat the oven to 350°F (180°C/Gas
   Mark 4).
3. Add the oysters to the frying pan and
   cook over a moderate heat for several
   minutes. Add the liquor and fold in the
   breadcrumbs.
4. Transfer the mixture to a greased
   casserole and sprinkle with the parmesan
   cheese. Bake for about 20 minutes, until
   the cheese is bubbly.

Calories per serving: 281
Calcium per serving: 337mg

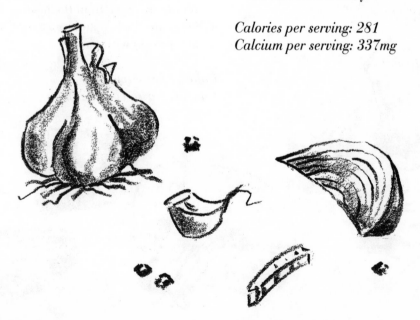

Pineapple Chicken

Serves 6

55g (2 oz) sliced unsalted almonds
1 large onion, finely chopped
750ml (1¼ pints) evaporated skimmed milk
110g (4 oz) tinned sliced mushrooms or
   fresh mushrooms, steamed
1 teaspoon salt
½ teaspoon freshly ground black pepper
pinch of ground ginger
450g (1 lb) tinned unsweetened pineapple
   chunks, drained
2 teaspoons cornflour
335g (12 oz) cooked skinless chicken, cubed
780g (28 oz) hot cooked rice
parsley to garnish

1. Toast the almonds in a large nonstick frying pan or wok. Remove the almonds from the pan and set aside.
2. Add the onions to the frying pan and cook until soft and golden brown, adding a little water to the pan if necessary. Reserve 120ml (4 fl oz) of the milk and add the remainder to the pan with the mushrooms, salt, pepper, ginger and pineapple. Stir-fry over a moderate heat until hot.
3. Dissolve the cornflour in the reserved milk, then add to the frying pan with the chicken and almonds. Bring the sauce to the boil, stirring constantly. Boil for 1 minute. Remove from the heat.
4. Serve the chicken and sauce over hot rice and garnish with parsley.

Calories per serving: 457
Calcium per serving: 427mg

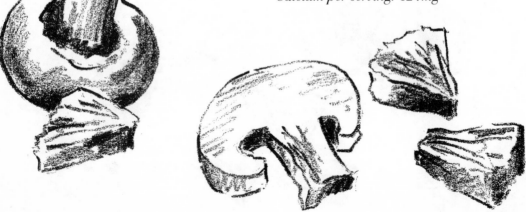

Poached Sole with Prawn Sauce

Serve with steamed rice.

Serves 4

1 tablespoon margarine
170g (6 oz) fresh mushrooms, sliced
juice of ½ lemon
salt
white pepper
450g (1 lb) Dover sole fillets
120ml (4 fl oz) dry white wine
1 bay leaf
110g (4 oz) cooked prawns
240ml (8 fl oz) White Wine Sauce (page 117)
parsley to garnish

1. Melt the margarine in a large frying pan and add the mushrooms, lemon juice and a pinch of salt. Stir-fry until the mushrooms are browned. Remove from the frying pan and set aside.
2. Season the fish fillets with salt and white pepper and fold each fillet in half. Arrange in one layer in the frying pan. Add the wine and bay leaf, cover and poach gently until the fish flakes easily, about 8-10 minutes.
3. Meanwhile, stir the mushrooms and prawns into the White Wine Sauce and heat thoroughly over a low heat.
4. When the fish is cooked, carefully remove it from the frying pan with a fish slice and transfer to a warmed serving dish. Pour the sauce over and garnish with parsley.

Calories per serving: 229
Calcium per serving: 237mg

Prawn and Cheese Soufflé

Serves 4

45g (1 oz) skimmed milk powder
240ml (8 fl oz) skimmed milk
2 tablespoons margarine
2 tablespoons cornflour
85g (3 oz) low fat processed cheddar cheese
3 eggs, separated
$\frac{1}{4}$ teaspoon cream of tartar
125g ($4\frac{1}{2}$ oz) prawns (if using tinned, rinse and drain)
$\frac{1}{2}$ teaspoon dried basil
1 teaspoon dried tarragon

1. Whisk the milk powder into the liquid milk until smooth; set aside.
2. Preheat the oven to 350°F (180°C/Gas Mark 4).
3. Grease a 1.5-litre ($3\frac{1}{2}$ pint) soufflé dish or casserole.
4. Melt the margarine in a saucepan over a low heat. Blend in the cornflour, stirring constantly, until the mixture is smooth and bubbly; remove from the heat. Stir in the milk and heat to boiling, stirring constantly. Stir in the cheese until melted; remove from the heat.
5. Whisk the egg whites and cream of tartar until stiff, but not dry. Whisk the egg yolks until very thick, about 5 minutes.
6. Add the prawns, basil, tarragon and egg yolks to the cheese mixture, stirring after each addition. Stir one-quarter of the egg whites into the cheese mixture to lighten it, then gently fold in the remaining egg whites.
7. Pour the mixture carefully into the prepared soufflé dish. Bake uncovered until a knife inserted halfway between the centre and edge comes out clean, about 50-60 minutes. Serve immediately.

Calories per serving: 236
Calcium per serving: 359mg

Salmon-Tofu Patties

As easy and delicious as hamburgers, these patties provide the perfect introduction for the tofuphobic cook.

Serves 6

390g (14 oz) firm tofu
195g (7 oz) tinned salmon, drained and
    flaked
2 egg whites
3 spring onions, finely chopped
pinch of black pepper

1. Wrap the tofu in a length of cheesecloth and squeeze out the excess moisture. Break the tofu up into small pieces and mix with the salmon, using either a fork or a food processor. Add the remaining ingredients and mix well. Form 6 hamburger-sized patties.
2. Brown the patties in a nonstick frying pan, about 5 minutes on each side.

Calories per serving: 124
Calcium per serving: 139mg

Tasty Stuffed Trout

Serves 4

75g (2½ oz) celery, finely chopped
30g (1 oz) tinned anchovies, finely chopped
    (reserve 2 teaspoons oil)
1 egg, beaten
85g (3 oz) dry breadcrumbs, mixed with
    ¾ teaspoon dried Italian seasoning
4 tablespoons grated parmesan cheese
85g (3 oz) skimmed milk powder
4 tablespoons finely chopped parsley
2 tablespoons lemon juice
4 whole trout (170-225g/6-8 oz each)
    gutted
salt
freshly ground black pepper
cherry tomatoes (optional) to garnish
parsley (optional) to garnish

1. Cook the celery in a nonstick saucepan with the anchovies and reserved oil until the celery is tender. Empty into a mixing bowl. Stir in the egg, seasoned breadcrumbs, cheese, skimmed milk powder, parsley and lemon juice.
2. Rub the cavities of the trout with salt and pepper and stuff with the breadcrumb mixture.
3. Preheat the oven to 350°F (180°C/Gas Mark 4).
4. Place the fish in a greased baking dish in one layer. Bake, uncovered until the fish flakes easily with a fork, about 30-35 minutes.
5. Garnish with cherry tomatoes and chopped parsley if desired.

Calories per serving: 515
Calcium per serving: 605mg

Tofu Vegetables

Serves 6

4 tablespoons low-sodium soy sauce
1 tablespoon sugar
$\frac{1}{2}$ teaspoon garlic powder
1 tablespoon cornflour
390g (14 oz) firm tofu, drained and cut into
   2cm ($\frac{3}{4}$-inch) cubes
120ml (4 fl oz) chicken or vegetable stock
2 stalks celery, sliced
3 spring onions, sliced
85g (3 oz) green pepper, chopped
110g (4 oz) fresh mushrooms, sliced
55g (2 oz) waterchestnuts, sliced
85g (3 oz) bamboo shoots, cut up
110g (4 oz) mangetout
55g (2 oz) sliced almonds
110g (4 oz) beansprouts

1. In a medium-sized bowl, mix together the soy sauce, sugar and garlic powder until dissolved. Blend in the cornstarch until smooth. Add the tofu and marinate for several hours, turning occasionally.
2. Bring the stock to the boil in a large nonstick frying pan. Add the celery, onions and pepper and simmer for 3 minutes, stirring occasionally. Add the mushrooms, waterchestnuts, bamboo shoots and mangetout and simmer for 2 minutes. Stir in the tofu cubes (reserving the marinade) and almonds and simmer for a further 2 minutes. Finally, add the bean sprouts and soy sauce mixture and stir for 1 minute. Serve immediately.

Calories per serving: 167
Calcium per serving: 121 mg

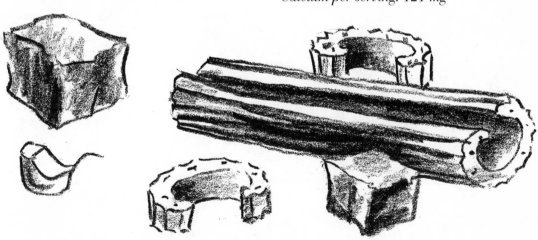

Turkey Taco Casserole

Serves 12

8 x 15cm (6-inch) corn tacos
785g (28 oz) minced raw turkey
1 onion, chopped
2 cloves garlic, crushed
$\frac{1}{2}$ tablespoon chilli powder
$\frac{1}{4}$ teaspoon ground cumin
$\frac{1}{4}$ teaspoon dried thyme
$\frac{1}{4}$ teaspoon salt
$\frac{1}{2}$ teaspoon dried oregano
450g (1 lb) mild cheddar cheese, grated
6 eggs, beaten
480ml (16 fl oz) skimmed milk
240ml (8 fl oz) natural yogurt
3 large tomatoes, chopped
225g (8 oz) lettuce, shredded
olives (optional)
salsa (optional) to serve

1. Preheat the oven to 350°F (180°C/Gas Mark 4).
2. Grease a 22.5 x 32.5cm (9 x 13 inch) baking dish and line with two layers of tortillas, breaking them to completely fill the base of the pan.
3. In a large frying pan, brown the turkey and onion, draining off the fat. Add the garlic, chilli powder, cumin, thyme, salt and oregano. Transfer the turkey mixture to the baking dish and top with the cheese, smoothing the layers evenly in the dish.
4. In a bowl, whisk the eggs with the milk and pour over the ingredients in the baking dish. Bake for 1 hour, or until the custard sets. Remove from the oven.
5. While the casserole is still warm, spread with the yogurt, then add the tomatoes, lettuce and olives, if using. Pass salsa at the table if desired.

Calories per serving: 378
Calcium per serving: 437mg

SIDE DISHES

Cheesy Noodle Scallop

Serves 8

500g (18 oz) tagliatelle
2 tablespoons cornflour
480ml (16 fl oz) skimmed milk
1 tablespoon margarine
85g (3 oz) onion, finely chopped
85g (3 oz) green pepper, finely chopped
½ teaspoon celery seed
225g (8 oz) feta cheese, crumbled
140g (5 oz) low fat cottage cheese
paprika

1. Cook tagliatelle according to the package directions. Drain well and set aside.
2. Mix the cornflour with a small quantity of the milk in a bowl. Blend until completely dissolved. Set aside.
3. Melt the margarine in a saucepan and cook the onion and green pepper until tender. Stir in the celery seed. Slowly add the remainder of the milk and the cornflour mixture and cook over a moderate heat, stirring constantly, until the sauce is thickened and boiling. Boil, stirring, for 1 minute. Fold in the feta and cottage cheese and remove from the heat.
4. Preheat the oven to 350°F (180°C/Gas Mark 4).
5. Combine the noodles and sauce and turn into a greased 2-litre (3½ pint) casserole. Sprinkle with paprika and bake, uncovered for 45 minutes.

Calories per serving: 247
Calcium per serving: 320mg

Creamy Mashed Potatoes

Serves 8

900g (2 lb) potatoes (about 6 medium
  sized)
approximately 120ml (4 fl oz) skimmed
  milk
85g (1½ oz) skimmed milk powder
55g (2 oz) low fat soft cheese, softened
½ teaspoon salt
pinch of freshly ground black pepper
½ teaspoon dried dillweed (optional)
parsley or chives (optional)

1. Wash and pare potatoes; remove any eyes.
   Cut into large chunks. Add 2.5cm (1
   inch) water in a saucepan and bring to
   the boil. Add the potatoes, bring to the
   boil again, then cover, reduce the heat
   and cook until tender, 20-25 minutes.
   Drain thoroughly. Shake the pan gently
   over a low heat to dry the potatoes, then
   remove from the heat.
2. Mash the potatoes in a bowl until smooth.
   Whisk in the liquid milk and milk powder
   in small amounts, alternating the two.
   (The amount of liquid milk needed
   depends on the type of potatoes used and
   the consistency desired.) Beat in the
   cream cheese, salt and pepper and dill, if
   using. Continue beating until the potatoes
   are light and fluffy.
3. Reheat over a very low heat or in a
   double boiler and sprinkle with chopped
   parsley or chives if desired.

Calories per serving: 156
Calcium per serving: 91mg

Gnocchi

Serves 8

720ml (24 fl oz) skimmed milk
125g ($4\frac{1}{2}$ oz) semolina
2 eggs, well-beaten
2 tablespoons low fat soft cheese
1 teaspoon garlic salt
pinch of freshly ground black pepper
15g ($\frac{1}{2}$ oz) margarine
70g ($2\frac{1}{2}$ oz) grated parmesan cheese

1. Heat milk to scalding in a 2-litre ($3\frac{1}{2}$ pint) saucepan; reduce heat to low. Sprinkle semolina slowly into the hot milk, stirring constantly. Cook until thick, about 5 minutes, stirring constantly. (The mixture will leave the sides of the pan when it is the right consistency.) Remove from the heat.
2. Stir in the eggs, soft cheese, garlic salt and pepper; beat until smooth. Grease a 22.5 x 32.5cm (9 x 13 inch) baking pan and spread the semolina mixture evenly into it. Cool, then refrigerate for 2-3 hours, until firm.
3. Cut the dough into 3.75cm ($1\frac{1}{2}$-inch) circles. (Dip the knife into cold water to prevent it from sticking.)
4. Preheat the oven to 350°F (180°C/Gas Mark 4).
5. Place the circles, overlapping, into an ungreased baking dish. Dot with the margarine and sprinkle with the parmesan cheese. Bake, uncovered until crisp and golden, about 45 minutes.

Calories per serving: 183
Calcium per serving: 336mg

Italian Rice and Peas

Serves 8

85g (3 oz) onion, chopped
240g (8½ oz) brown rice
630ml (21 fl oz) water
2 chicken bouillon cubes
280g (10 oz) frozen peas, cooked and
    drained
85g (3 oz) parmesan cheese

1. Brown the onion and rice in a nonstick saucepan, stirring occasionally. Stir in the water and the bouillon cubes and bring to the boil, stirring once or twice. Reduce the heat to as low as possible, cover the pan and simmer until the rice is tender and the liquid is absorbed, about 30-40 minutes. Remove from the heat.
2. Gently stir in the peas; cover and set aside for 5-10 minutes. Fork in the cheese lightly, then serve immediately.

Calories per serving: 188
Calcium per serving: 125mg

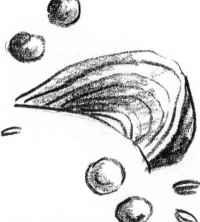
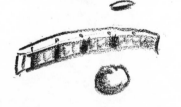

Oyster Stuffing

This light side dish won't leave you 'stuffed'—it has no added fat!

Serves 4

125g (4½ oz) onion, finely chopped
125g (4½ oz) celery, finely chopped, with leaves
125 (4½ oz) soft bread, cubed
150 ml (¼ pint) evaporated skimmed milk
225g (8 oz) tinned oysters, drained and chopped
1 teaspoon salt
¾ teaspoon dried sage
½ teaspoon dried thyme
¼ teaspoon freshly ground black pepper

1. Preheat the oven to 325°F (160°C/Gas Mark 3).
2. Place the onion and celery in a nonstick frying pan and stir-fry until the onion is tender. Remove from the heat.
3. Turn the onion-celery mixture into a large bowl. Mix in all the remaining ingredients thoroughly.
4. Grease a 1.5 litre (2½ pint) casserole. Spoon the stuffing mixture in; cover and bake for 1 hour. Uncover for the last 15 minutes to brown the stuffing if desired.

Calories per serving: 149
Calcium per serving: 203mg

Potato Casserole

Serves 8

900g (2 lb) potatoes (about 6 medium
  sized)
freshly ground black pepper
1 teaspoon garlic salt
3 tablespoons chopped parsley
1 small onion, chopped
110g (4 oz) low fat processed cheddar
  cheese, thinly sliced or grated
240ml (8 fl oz) evaporated whole milk

1. Wash and pare potatoes, removing any
   eyes. Cut into strips lengthways, about
   .75cm ($\frac{1}{4}$-inch) wide.
2. Preheat the oven to 350°F (180°C/Gas
   Mark 4).
3. Arrange the potatoes in a greased
   casserole in 3 layers, topping each layer
   with a grinding of pepper and one-third
   each of the garlic salt, parsley, onion and
   cheese. Pour the evaporated milk over.
   Cover and bake for 60-70 minutes, until
   the potatoes are tender.

Calories per serving: 200
Calcium per serving: 197mg

Special Stuffed Potatoes

A delicious complement to a classic main course dish, such as poached fish or roast beef.

Serves 6

4 spring onions, chopped
110g (4 oz) fresh mushrooms, sliced
150ml ($\frac{1}{4}$ pint) evaporated skimmed milk
110g (4 oz) gruyère cheese, grated
110g (4 oz) feta cheese, crumbled
125g (4$\frac{1}{2}$ oz) prawns, fresh or frozen
6 jacket potatoes, baked, with the pulp
    spooned out and reserved
$\frac{1}{4}$ teaspoon salt
pinch of cayenne pepper
paprika

1. Steam the spring onions and mushrooms with a small amount of water in a nonstick saucepan until the vegetables are tender and the mushrooms are browned. Remove from the heat and add the milk.
2. Return to a low heat and whisk in the cheeses, a little at a time. When the cheeses are melted, stir in the prawns, potato pulp, salt and pepper.
3. Stuff the potato skins with the mixture and sprinkle with paprika.
4. Heat the grill and grill the stuffed potatoes for 3 minutes. Serve immediately.

Calories per serving: 318
Calcium per serving: 440mg

Tex-Mex Rice and Cheese

Serves 8

590g (21 oz) cooked rice
480ml (16 fl oz) natural yogurt
1½ teaspoons garlic salt
1 teaspoon onion powder
225g (8 oz) mild cheddar cheese, sliced
170g (6 oz) tinned whole peeled chillies,
    drained and chopped, divided

1. Preheat the oven to 325°F (160°C/Gas
   Mark 3).
2. In a bowl, combine rice, yogurt, garlic
   salt and onion powder.
3. Arrange half of the rice mixture in a
   greased 2-litre (3½ pint) casserole. Top
   with half each of the cheese and chillies.
   Spread the remaining rice mixture on top,
   then the remaining cheese and chillies.
4. Bake for 30 minutes.

Calories per serving: 226
Calcium per serving: 319mg

Two-Step Rice and Beans

A savoury side dish for Spanish omelettes.

Serves 6

170g (6 oz) onions, chopped
840g (30 oz) tinned kidney beans, drained
390g (14 oz) cooked rice
225 g (8 oz) tomato sauce
3 tablespoons imitation bacon bits
    (optional)
55g (2 oz) muscovado sugar
1 teaspoon prepared mustard
½ tablespoon salt
¼ teaspoon freshly ground black pepper

1. Cook onion in a nonstick saucepan until
   tender, but not browned. Stir in the
   remaining ingredients. Cover and simmer
   for about 10 minutes.

Calories per serving: 257
Calcium per serving: 66mg

VEGETABLES

Colourful Vegetable Bake _____

Serves 12

125g (4½ oz) carrots, sliced
170g (6 oz) runner beans, cut into 4cm (1½ -
   inch) lengths
390g (14 oz) firm tofu, drained
450g (14 oz) tinned whole tomatoes,
   drained
170g (6 oz) frozen sweetcorn, thawed and
   drained
2 cloves garlic, finely chopped
½ teaspoon salt
pinch of freshly ground black pepper
30g (1 oz) chopped blanched almonds

1. Preheat the oven to 375°F (190°C/Gas
   Mark 5).
2. If you prefer your vegetables not to be
   crunchy, steam the carrots and runner
   beans for 5 minutes; otherwise, proceed
   with the recipe.
3. Cut the tofu into 1.25cm (½ -inch) cubes
   and cut the tomatoes into quarters.
   Combine all ingredients except the
   almonds in a large bowl and mix
   thoroughly.
4. Turn the vegetable mixture into a greased
   2-litre (3½ pint) casserole. Top with the
   almonds and bake, uncovered until the
   vegetables are tender, about 30-40
   minutes.

Calories per serving: 64
Calcium per serving: 69mg

Spaghetti Squash Mozzarella _____

Spaghetti squash is a large, oblong yellow marrow that separates into spaghetti-like strands after it has been cooked.

Serves 8

½ spaghetti squash, cut lengthways
55g (2 oz) mozzarella cheese, grated
1 tablespoon grated parmesan cheese
3 tablespoons seasoned dry breadcrumbs
1 teaspoon garlic powder
1 tablespoon chopped parsley

1. Preheat the oven to 350°F (180°C/Gas Mark 4).
2. Scoop out the squash seeds and discard. Place the squash, cut side down, in a saucepan containing 5cm (2 inches) water. Cover and boil for 20 minutes. Remove from the water and drain.
3. With a fork, remove the strands of squash and transfer to a bowl. In another bowl, combine the remaining ingredients and mix well. Blend this mixture into the squash.
4. Transfer the squash to a casserole dish and bake, uncovered until the cheese melts and the casserole is slightly browned, about 20 minutes.

Calories per serving: 42
Calcium per serving: 82mg

Pak Choi with Mushrooms

Also known as Chinese mustard cabbage, this vegetable has large, dark green leaves and long white stems. The stalks are stringless, crunchy and mild in flavour.

Serves 6

560g (1¼ lb) pak choi
1 chicken bouillon cube
180ml (6 fl oz) boiling water
1 tablespoon cornflour
1 teaspoon sugar
¼ teaspoon ground ginger
1 tablespoon soy sauce
15g (½ oz) margarine
85g (3 oz) onion, chopped
110g (4 oz) fresh mushrooms, sliced
1 medium-sized carrot, sliced diagonally
1 clove garlic, finely chopped

1. Cut the pak choi lengthways through the stalk, then crossways into slices about 1.25cm (½ inch).
2. Combine the bouillon cube and boiling water in a jug; stir to dissolve.
3. Mix the cornflour, sugar, ginger, soy sauce and half of the stock together well in a cup.
4. Melt the margarine in a nonstick frying pan or wok. Add the onion and sauté for 2 minutes. Remove from the wok and set aside. Add the pak choi, carrot, garlic and the unmixed half of the stock to the wok and stir-fry for 2 minutes. Stir in the cornflour mixture. Cook and stir until the mixture thickens and boils. Reduce the heat and simmer, covered until the vegetables are tender, about 3 minutes. Return the onion and mushrooms to the wok and heat until hot.

Calories per serving: 58
Calcium per serving: 168mg

Broccoli Stir-Fry

A classic Chinese dish.

Serves 4

450g (1 lb) broccoli
1 tablespoon vegetable oil
1 garlic clove, crushed
$\frac{1}{2}$ teaspoon salt
1 teaspoon rice wine or sherry
$\frac{1}{4}$ teaspoon sugar
3 tablespoons chicken stock
$\frac{1}{4}$ cup water

1. Rinse broccoli under the cold tap. Dry. Cut into 5cm (2-inch) florets and stems approximately .75cm ($\frac{1}{4}$ inch) thick.
2. Heat the oil in a nonstick frying pan or wok over high heat for 30 seconds. Stir-fry the garlic until golden, about 30 seconds. Add broccoli stems and salt. Stir-fry for 30 seconds. Add broccoli florets. Stir-fry 1 minute. Add the wine, sugar, stock and water. Reduce the heat to medium-low and continue to stir-fry until the liquid is almost gone. Serve hot.

Calories per serving: 53
Calcium per serving: 69mg

Creamed Turnip Greens

Although turnip greens are not sold in supermarkets, some greengrocers are able to obtain them, or you might be fortunate enough to have a farmer friend! If not, you can always substitute another dark green leafy vegetable.

Serves 12

1 large onion, chopped
2 stalks celery, chopped
675g (1½ lb) fresh turnip greens, or
    substitute spring greens, kale or spinach
1 tablespoon cornflour
360ml (12 fl oz) evaporated skimmed milk
1 teaspoon garlic powder
½ teaspoon salt
1 teaspoon sugar
pinch of freshly ground black pepper
2 tablespoons imitation bacon bits
    (optional)

1. Cook the onion and celery in a nonstick saucepan until tender; set aside.
2. Remove the root ends and imperfect leaves from the turnip greens and wash thoroughly.
3. Cook the greens, covered in a small amount of boiling water until tender, about 15-20 minutes.
4. Meanwhile, blend the cornflour into the milk; add garlic powder, salt, sugar and pepper. Cook in a small saucepan over a low heat, stirring constantly, until thickened to the consistency of condensed tinned cream soup.
5. Preheat the oven to 350°F (180°C/Gas Mark 4)
6. Drain the greens and combine with the sauce, onion and celery. Turn into an ungreased baking dish, sprinkle bacon bits on top, if using, and bake until browned, about 25-30 minutes.

Calories per serving: 58
Calcium per serving: 196mg

Salted Spinach Sauté

Serves 3

450g (1 lb) fresh spinach
30g (1 oz) tinned anchovies, drained and
  chopped
1 small onion, thinly sliced
pinch of freshly ground black pepper

1. Remove the root ends and imperfect
   leaves from the spinach. Wash thoroughly
   and drain.
2. Stir-fry the anchovies and onion in a large
   nonstick frying pan until the onion is
   tender. Add about half the spinach and
   the pepper. Cover and cook over a
   moderate heat for about 2 minutes. Add
   the remaining spinach. Cover and cook,
   stirring occasionally, until the spinach is
   tender, 3-10 minutes.

Calories per serving: 47
Calcium per serving: 108mg

Swiss Vegetables

This colourful and tasty combination might even appeal to the vegetable haters in your family.

Serves 8

1 tablespoon cornflour
300ml ($\frac{1}{2}$ pint) evaporated skimmed milk
450g (1 lb) frozen broccoli, carrot and cauliflower combination, thawed and drained
110g (4 oz) tinned mushrooms, drained
85g (3 oz) gruyère cheese, grated
55g (2 oz) seasoned breadcrumbs, divided
75ml (2$\frac{1}{2}$ fl oz) natural yogurt
$\frac{1}{4}$ teaspoon salt
$\frac{1}{4}$ teaspoon freshly ground black pepper

1. Preheat the oven to 350°F (180°C/Gas Mark 4).
2. Add cornflour to the milk slowly and blend thoroughly. Cook in a saucepan over a low heat until boiling, stirring constantly. Stir and boil 1 minute. Add vegetables, two-thirds of the cheese, half the breadcrumbs, yogurt, salt and pepper to the cornflour mixture and blend well.
3. Turn the mixture into a 1.5 litre (2$\frac{1}{2}$ pint) casserole. Bake, covered for 30 minutes. Mix together the remaining cheese and breadcrumbs and sprinkle on top of casserole. Bake for a further 5 minutes.

Calories per serving: 121
Calcium per serving: 262mg

SAUCES, DRESSINGS AND DIPS

Blue Cheese Dip

Makes approximately 1 litre (1½ pints)

600ml (1 pint) natural yogurt
335g (12 oz) reduced-calorie mayonnaise
85g (3 oz) onion, chopped
170g (6 oz) blue cheese, finely crumbled
pinch of salt
½ teaspoon garlic powder
1-2 tablespoons chopped parsley

1. Mix the yogurt and mayonnaise together in a bowl. Add remaining ingredients and mix well.
2. Serve cold with cut raw vegetables or crisp plain biscuits, or use as a salad dressing. This dip can also be heated in a microwave oven and served with baked corn tortillas or tortilla chips.

Calories per serving: 24 per tablespoon
Calcium per serving: 32mg per tablespoon

Cooked Salad Dressing

Makes about 450ml (¾ pint)

5 tablespoons plain flour
1½ tablespoons sugar
1 teaspoon salt
1 teaspoon mustard powder
360ml (12 fl oz) skimmed milk
2 egg yolks, slightly beaten
75ml (2½ fl oz) rice vinegar

1. Mix the flour, salt and mustard powder together in a 2-litre (3½ pint) saucepan. Stir in the milk gradually and bring to the boil over a moderate heat, stirring constantly. Boil and stir 1 minute. Remove from the heat.
2. Gradually stir at least half the milk mixture into the egg yolks, then return the mixture to the saucepan. Boil and stir 1 minute. Remove from the heat and stir in the vinegar. Cool slightly, then refrigerate.

Calories per serving: 17 per tablespoon
Calcium per serving: 20mg per tablespoon

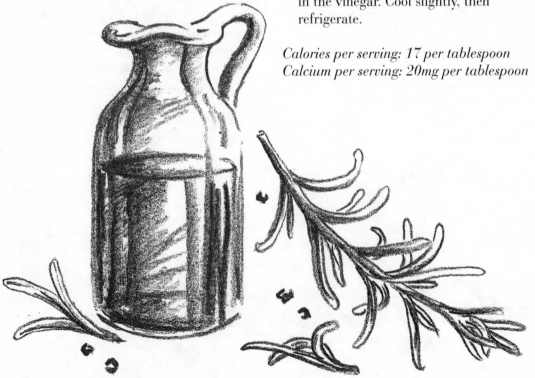

Clam Sauce

Serves 4

365g (13 oz) tinned clams, chopped
150ml ($\frac{1}{4}$ pint) clam liquor (reserved from tinned clams)
$\frac{1}{2}$ tablespoon cornflour
1 tablespoon olive oil
15g ($\frac{1}{2}$ oz) margarine
1 small onion, finely chopped
2 small cloves garlic, finely chopped
salt and ground white pepper
$\frac{1}{4}$ teaspoon dried oregano
225g (8 oz) linguine, cooked, to serve
chopped parsley to serve
grated parmesan cheese to serve

1. Drain the clams reserving 150ml ($\frac{1}{4}$ pint) of the liquor. Add cornflour to the clam liquor and blend well.
2. Heat the olive oil and margarine in a saucepan; add the onion, garlic, salt and pepper to taste and cook until golden. Add the oregano, chopped clams and clam liquor mixture. Stir over a low heat until thickened. Increase the heat and bring to the boil. Boil 1 minute. Remove from the heat.
3. Serve hot over cooked linguine; sprinkle with chopped parsley and parmesan cheese.

Calories per serving: 129
Calcium per serving: 75mg

Spicy Yogurt Dressing

This salad dressing is not for the faint of palate!

Makes approximately 300ml (½ pint)

240ml (8 fl oz) natural yogurt
2 tablespoons lemon juice
1 tablespoon sugar
85g (3 oz) skimmed milk powder
½ teaspoon salt
¼ teaspoon ground cumin
pinch of freshly ground black pepper
pinch of cayenne pepper

1. Put the yogurt in a small mixing bowl. Beat with a fork until smooth and creamy. Stir in the lemon juice, sugar, and skimmed milk powder and blend until smooth. Add the salt, cumin, black pepper and cayenne pepper and mix well.
2. Refrigerate in a covered container.

Calories per serving: 32 per 2 tablespoons
Calcium per serving: 84mg per 2 tablespoons

Spinach Spread

This is a favourite in the Fredal household.

Makes approximately 750ml (1¼ pints)

560g (20 oz) frozen chopped spinach, thawed and squeezed dry
8 tablespoons reduced-calorie mayonnaise
360ml (12 fl oz) natural yogurt
1 sachet Knorr vegetable soup mix
2 spring onions, finely chopped

1. Mix all ingredients together thoroughly by hand or with an electric whisk.
2. Refrigerate in a covered container overnight before serving to blend flavours.

Calories per serving: 25 per 2 tablespoons
Calcium per serving: 49mg per 2 tablespoons

Tahini Dipping Sauce

Tahini—sesame seed paste—can be purchased in Middle Eastern or health food shops.

Makes about 360ml (12 fl oz)

5 cloves garlic, finely chopped
1 teaspoon salt
8 tablespoons tahini (sesame seed paste)
120ml (4 fl oz) lemon juice
60ml (2 fl oz) cold water

1. Crush the garlic and salt into a paste. Add to the tahini in a small bowl and beat together with a fork. Add lemon juice and water, one at a time, beating constantly until well-blended.

Calories per serving: 62 per 2 tablespoons
Calcium per serving: 27mg per 2 tablespoons

Tangy Cheese Sauce

Makes approximately 450ml ($\frac{3}{4}$ pint)

1 tablespoon margarine
1 tablespoon cornflour
1 teaspoon prepared mustard
$\frac{1}{4}$ teaspoon salt
pinch of freshly ground black pepper
300ml ($\frac{1}{2}$ pint) skimmed milk
110g (4 oz) low fat processed cheddar cheese, diced
5 drops Tabasco

1. Melt margarine in a saucepan over low heat. Blend in cornflour, mustard, salt and pepper. Cook, stirring constantly, until the mixture is smooth; remove from the heat.
2. Stir in the milk, then return to a low heat and cook until thickened, stirring constantly. Stir in the cheese and hot pepper sauce. Cook, stirring, until the cheese is melted.
3. Serve over steamed broccoli or cauliflower, or over warm cornbread.

Calories per serving: 29 per 2 tablespoons
Calcium per serving: 78mg per 2 tablespoons

Yogurt Cheese

A great low-calorie substitute for full-fat soft cheese! Plain or sweetened, yogurt cheese goes well with fresh fruit, or it can be used as a spread for rolls or scones. The savoury variety can be spread on bread or plain biscuits.

Makes approximately 110g (4 oz)

240ml (8 fl oz) natural low fat yogurt

Flavourings: (optional)

Savoury:
$\frac{1}{2}$ tablespoon finely chopped parsley
pinch of salt
$\frac{1}{2}$ tablespoon finely sliced chives

Sweet:
1 tablespoon apple purée or orange
 marmalade

1. Place the yogurt in the centre of a treble thickness square of cheesecloth, large enough to be hung. Bring the corners of the cheesecloth together and tie securely. Suspend in a place where it can drip, for example, tie to the tap of the kitchen sink. Allow to drip for 8 hours or overnight.
2. Remove the cheese from the cheesecloth and transfer to a closed plastic container. (If you are adding flavourings, mix them into the yogurt cheese before refrigerating.) Refrigerate well before using.

Calories per serving:
Savoury—18 per tablespoon
Sweet—22 per tablespoon
Calcium per serving: 52mg per tablespoon

White Wine Sauce

Excellent with poached fish.

Makes 240ml (8 fl oz)

1 tablespoon margarine
2 small shallots, finely chopped
1 tablespoon cornflour
75ml (2½ fl oz) dry white wine
150ml (¼ pint) evaporated skimmed milk
¼ teaspoon salt
pinch of white pepper

1. Melt the margarine in a small saucepan. Add the shallots and cook until lightly browned. Stir in the cornflour. Add the wine, milk, salt and pepper and cook over a low heat until thickened, stirring constantly. Do not boil. When the sauce is of the desired consistency, increase the heat and bring to a light boil; then remove from the heat.

Calories per serving: 42 per 2 tablespoons
Calcium per serving: 67mg per 2 tablespoons

BREADS

Almond-Fruit Bread

Makes one 900g (2-lb) loaf: 16 slices

55g (2 oz) margarine, softened
110g (4 oz) sugar
2 teaspoons grated lemon rind
$\frac{1}{2}$ teaspoon ground cinnamon
2 eggs
3 tablespoons skimmed milk
1 teaspoon lemon juice
185g ($6\frac{1}{2}$ oz) plain flour
85g (3 oz) skimmed milk powder
$\frac{1}{2}$ tablespoon baking powder
1 teaspoon salt
$\frac{1}{4}$ teaspoon bicarbonate of soda
140g (5 oz) apple, peeled and grated
140g (5 oz) dried figs, chopped
55g (2 oz) almonds, chopped

1. Preheat the oven to 350°F (180°C/Gas Mark 4).
2. Cream the margarine, sugar, lemon rind and cinnamon together in a large mixing bowl with an electric whisk. Add the eggs and whisk until light and fluffy. Whisk in the milk and lemon juice.
3. Mix the flour, skimmed milk powder, baking powder, salt and bicarbonate of soda together thoroughly and add to the creamed mixture until just moistened. Do not overmix. Fold in the apple, figs and almonds.
4. Pour the batter into a 1 kilo (2-lb) loaf tin and bake for 1 hour, or until a wooden cocktail stick inserted into the centre comes out clean.

Calories per serving: 171 per slice
Calcium per serving: 61mg per slice

Hearty Flat Bread

One version of an Indian staple, this bread will complement a thick soup or chowder.

Makes 9 small loaves

185g (6½ oz) wholemeal flour
185g (6½ oz) plain flour
1½ tablespoons baking powder
½ teaspoon salt
85g (3 oz) skimmed milk powder
420ml (14 fl oz) natural yogurt

1. Sift the flours, baking powder, salt and skimmed milk powder into a bowl.
2. With your hands, slowly mix in as much yogurt as is needed to make a soft, resilient dough. Knead about 10-15 minutes and form dough into a ball. Put dough into a bowl, cover with a damp cloth and set aside in a warm place for 1½ -2 hours.
3. Divide the dough into 9 equal parts and keep them covered with the cloth.
4. Heat a frying pan or griddle over a medium-low heat. Preheat the grill.
5. Form one of the portions of dough into a ball and roll out until it is about .3cm (⅛ inch) thick. When the frying pan is very hot, put the dough circle on it. Cook slowly for 4-5 minutes until it is partially puffed up. Then remove with a spatula and put under the grill for about 1 minute, until there are a few reddish-brown spots on top. Remove from the grill and cover with a clean cloth. Continue until all 9 loaves are cooked.
6. To reheat the bread, wrap in aluminium foil and heat in a 400°F (200°C/Gas Mark 6) oven for 15 minutes.

Calories per serving: 201 per loaf
Calcium per serving: 175mg per loaf

Apple-Oat Bran Muffins

Oat bran, a soluble fibre, helps to lower blood sugar and cholesterol levels.

Makes 12 muffins

110g (4 oz) wholemeal flour
170g (6 oz) oat bran
$2\frac{1}{2}$ teaspoons baking powder
1 teaspoon salt
$\frac{1}{4}$ teaspoon bicarbonate of soda
55g (2 oz) muscovado sugar
85g (3 oz) skimmed milk powder
1 teaspoon ground cinnamon
$\frac{1}{2}$ teaspoon freshly grated nutmeg
3 tablespoons vegetable oil
240ml (8 fl oz) natural yogurt
1 egg
180g ($6\frac{1}{2}$ oz) unsweetened apple purée

1. Preheat the oven to 400°F (200°C/Gas Mark 6).
2. In a large bowl, mix the flour, oat bran, baking powder, salt, bicarbonate of soda, sugar, skimmed milk powder, cinnamon and nutmeg together thoroughly.
3. In a separate bowl, whisk the oil, yogurt and egg together. Blend in the apple purée. Add the wet ingredients to the dry and blend until just moistened; do not overmix.
4. Grease a 12-cup muffin tin or insert cake liners. Pour the batter into the cups, filling them two-thirds full.
5. Bake for 20 minutes, or until golden-brown.

Calories per serving: 158 per muffin
Calcium per serving: 141mg per muffin

Cornbread

Makes 16 squares

250g (9 oz) cornmeal
55g (2 oz) wholemeal flour
55g (2 oz) plain flour
85g (3 oz) skimmed milk powder
4 teaspoons baking powder
$\frac{1}{4}$ teaspoon bicarbonate of soda
$\frac{1}{2}$ teaspoon salt
1 egg
300ml ($\frac{1}{2}$ pint) skimmed milk
60ml (2 fl oz) vegetable oil
170g (6 oz) clear honey
1 teaspoon vanilla essence

1. Preheat the oven to 375°F (190°C/Gas Mark 5).
2. In a large bowl, sift together thoroughly the cornmeal, flours, skimmed milk powder, baking powder, bicarbonate of soda and salt.
3. In a separate bowl, whisk together the egg, milk, oil, honey and vanilla essence. Add the wet ingredients to the dry ingredients and mix until just moistened. Do not overmix.
4. Pour the batter into a greased 22.5cm (9-inch) square tin and bake for 30-35 minutes, until golden-brown.

Calories per serving: 173 per square
Calcium per serving 112mg per square

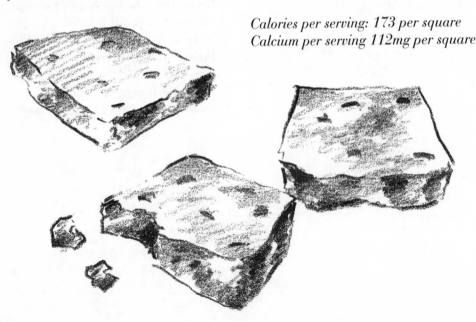

Currant Scones

Makes 12 scones

185g (6½ oz) plain flour
2 tablespoons sugar
2½ teaspoons baking powder
85g (3 oz) skimmed milk powder
½ teaspoon salt
55g (2 oz) cold margarine
2 eggs, beaten
75ml (2½ fl oz) evaporated skimmed milk
55g (2 oz) dried currants

1. Preheat the oven to 425°F (220°C/Gas Mark 7).
2. In a large bowl, sift together the flour, sugar, baking powder, skimmed milk powder and salt. Cut the margarine in with two knives or a pastry blender until the margarine is the size of small peas.
3. Reserve 1 tablespoon of the beaten egg. To the remainder, whisk in the liquid milk.
4. Make a well in the centre of the dry ingredients; pour the liquid and the currants in and combine the ingredients with swift strokes of a fork until the dough holds together and leaves the sides of the bowl.
5. Turn the dough out on to a lightly floured board and roll it out to a thickness of 2cm (¾ inch). Cut out circles in the dough with a floured 5cm (2-inch) biscuit cutter, re-rolling the scraps—you should have 12 dough circles.
6. Place the scones on an ungreased baking sheet, brush with the reserved egg and bake until golden, about 12-15 minutes.

Calories per serving: 146 per scone
Calcium per serving: 120mg per scone

Irish Soda Loaf

This quick and easy bread is not only delicious, but brings an old-fashioned aroma to today's busy kitchen.

Makes 16 slices

225g (8 oz) plain flour
100g (3½ oz) skimmed milk powder
1 teaspoon bicarbonate of soda
1 teaspoon baking powder
½ teaspoon salt
2 tablespoons sugar
45g (1½ oz) margarine, softened
55g (2 oz) seedless raisins
240ml (8 fl oz) natural yogurt

1. Preheat the oven to 375°F (190°C/Gas Mark 5).
2. In a large bowl, sift together the flour, skimmed milk powder, bicarbonate of soda, baking powder, salt and sugar. Cut in the margarine until the mixture resembles fine breadcrumbs. Stir in the raisins and enough yogurt to make a soft dough.
3. Turn the dough out on to a lightly floured board and knead until smooth, 1-2 minutes. Shape into a round loaf about 16cm (6½ inches) in diameter.
4. Place the loaf on a greased baking sheet. Cut an X about one-quarter deep in the centre of the loaf with a floured knife. Bake until golden-brown, about 35 minutes.

Calories per serving: 110 per slice
Calcium per serving: 70mg per slice

Pancakes à l'Orange

Makes 4 pancakes

5 tablespoons wholemeal flour
3 tablespoons skimmed milk powder
1 teaspoon baking powder
pinch of salt
$\frac{1}{2}$ orange, separated into segments and
   finely cut (including the juice)
90ml (3 fl oz) orange juice

1. In a bowl, sift the flour, skimmed milk powder, baking powder and salt together.
2. Stir in the orange segments and orange juice and mix just until the dry ingredients are moistened. Do not overmix.
3. Heat a nonstick griddle or frying pan. When it is very hot, spoon one-quarter of the batter on to the griddle for each pancake. Cook over moderate heat until the underside is golden. Flip and cook until golden-brown.

Calories per serving: 62 per pancake
Calcium per serving: 104mg per pancake

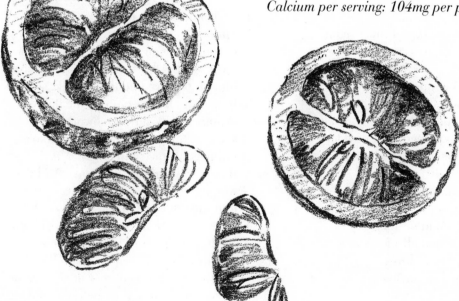

Pumpkin Bread

In America, one can buy tinned pumpkin purée and ground pumpkin pie spice. Since these are not available in the UK, we have altered the original recipe slightly—Publisher's note.

Pumpkin purée
1 medium pumpkin, with the seeds removed

Makes two 900g (2-lb) loaves: 32 slices

Calories per serving: 151 per slice
Calcium per serving: 59mg per slice

75ml (2½ fl oz) vegetable oil
310g (11 oz) soft dark brown sugar
1 teaspoon vanilla essence
4 eggs, beaten
16 oz pumpkin purée (see above)
240ml (8 fl oz) skimmed milk
390g (14 oz) plain flour
100g (3½ oz) skimmed milk powder
2 teaspoons bicarbonate of soda
½ tablespoon salt
½ teaspoon baking powder
1 teaspoon ground cinnamon
½ teaspoon ground nutmeg
½ teaspoon ground allspice
1 teaspoon ground cloves
85g (3 oz) seedless raisins

1. Discard the pumpkin seeds (or dry them and add to bread ingredients). Cut the pumpkin flesh into chunks.
2. Cook the pumpkin in a saucepan in boiling salted water until very tender, about 15-20 minutes. Remove from the water with a slotted spoon, drain and cool slightly.
3. Purée the pumpkin in a food processor or blender until very smooth.
4. Freeze in 1lb quantities.

1. Preheat the oven to 350°F (180°C/Gas Mark 4).
2. Combine the oil and brown sugar in a large bowl. Add the vanilla essence, eggs, pumpkin purée and liquid milk.
3. In another bowl, combine the flour, skimmed milk powder, bicarbonate of soda, salt, baking powder, cinnamon, nutmeg, allspice and cloves. Mix thoroughly and stir in raisins. Add the wet ingredients to the dry ones and mix until just moistened. Do not overmix.
4. Pour the batter into two greased 1-kilo (2-lb) loaf tins and bake for about 70 minutes, until a wooden cocktail stick inserted into the centre of the loaf comes out clean. Cool slightly before removing from pans.

Strawberry-Cheese Crêpes

Sunday morning at Judy's house often meant Dad's delicious crêpes. This version is filled with cottage cheese for extra calcium and protein.

Serves 8

360ml (12 fl oz) low fat milk
15g ($\frac{1}{2}$ oz) margarine
3 eggs, beaten
110g (4 oz) plain flour
$\frac{1}{2}$ teaspoon salt
vegetable oil to grease
310g (11 oz) fresh or frozen strawberries,
   crushed (if using frozen, thaw completely)
1 teaspoon sugar
225g (8 oz) low fat cottage cheese

1. Heat the milk and margarine in a small saucepan until the margarine melts. Remove from the heat and transfer to a mixing bowl.
2. Add the eggs, flour and salt and whisk with an electric whisk until smooth.
3. Dip a bit of absorbent kitchen paper into the vegetable oil and wipe a nonstick frying pan thoroughly, leaving only the slightest film of oil. Heat the pan over a moderate heat.
4. Pour only enough batter to coat the base of the pan, tilting the pan to coat evenly. Cook until browned on the underside, about 1 minute. Turn the crêpe and brown the other side. Remove from the pan, place on a warmed serving plate and continue making the crêpes until all the batter is used up.
5. Sprinkle the strawberries with the sugar. Spread $1\frac{1}{2}$ -2 tablespoons cottage cheese on each crêpe and roll up. Top each with 2-3 tablespoons strawberries.

Calories per serving: 213
Calcium per serving: 106mg

Wholegrain Muffins

High in fibre and complex carbohydrates, one of these muffins and a frothy breakfast shake will start your day out right.

Makes 12 muffins

85g (3 oz) wholewheat flake cereal
360ml (12 fl oz) skimmed milk
1 egg, beaten
75ml (2½ fl oz) vegetable oil
170g (6 oz) wholemeal flour
110g (4 oz) sugar
85g (3 oz) skimmed milk powder
4½ teaspoons baking powder
1 teaspoon salt

1. Preheat the oven to 375°F (190°C/Gas Mark 5). Grease a 12-cup muffin tin or line with paper cases.
2. Measure the cereal by filling a 600ml (1 pint) measuring jug. Combine with the milk in a mixing bowl and allow to stand 5 minutes, or until the cereal is softened. Add the egg and oil and beat together well.
3. In another bowl, mix the flour, sugar, skimmed milk powder, baking powder and salt together thoroughly. Add the dry ingredients to the wet ones and mix only until just moistened. (The mixture will be lumpy.)
4. Fill the prepared muffin cups two-thirds full and bake for 20-30 minutes or until the muffins are lightly browned. Remove from the oven and cool slightly.

Calories per serving: 187 per muffin
Calcium per serving: 123mg per muffin

DESSERTS

Easy Yogurt Pie

Serves 6

480ml (16 fl oz) low fat fruit yogurt
 (strawberry, raspberry, etc.)
85g (3 oz) fresh or unsweetened frozen fruit
 (use the same flavour as the yogurt),
 thawed if frozen
180ml (6 fl oz) evaporated whole milk,
 chilled
1 teaspoon lemon juice
2 tablespoons sugar
1 teaspoon vanilla essence
1 baked crumb crust (see recipe for cottage
 cheesecake, page 131)

Also needed:
chilled metal bowl
chilled whisks

1. In a bowl, mix the yogurt and fresh or
 thawed frozen fruit thoroughly.
2. Pour the chilled evaporated milk into the
 chilled bowl and whisk with chilled
 beaters until foamy. Add the lemon juice
 and whisk until firm. Add the sugar and
 vanilla essence and whip until stiff. Fold
 the whipped milk thoroughly into the
 yogurt mixture.
3. Spoon into the prepared crust and freeze
 for 4 hours.
4. Transfer from the freezer to the
 refrigerator 30 minutes before serving (or
 earlier if you prefer a softer texture).
 Store in the freezer.

Calories per serving: 316
Calcium per serving: 211mg

Almond Coffee Cake

Serves 16

225g (8 oz) sugar
70g (2½ oz) margarine, softened
3 eggs
½ tablespoon vanilla essence
335g (12 oz) almond paste
335g (12 oz) wholemeal flour
2 teaspoons baking powder
85g (3 oz) skimmed milk powder
½ tablespoon bicarbonate of soda
½ teaspoon salt
360ml (12 fl oz) natural yogurt
50g (1¾ oz) icing sugar
2 teaspoons warm milk

1. Preheat the oven to 350°F (180°C/Gas Mark 4). Grease a 30cm (10-inch) tube tin.
2. Beat the sugar, margarine, eggs and vanilla essence in a large mixing bowl with an electric mixer on medium speed for about 2 minutes, scraping the bowl occasionally with a rubber scraper. Beat in the almond paste.
3. In another bowl, combine the flour, baking powder, skimmed milk powder, bicarbonate of soda and salt; blend into the egg mixture alternately with the yogurt.
4. Pour the batter into the prepared tin and bake for approximately 1 hour, until a wooden cocktail stick inserted into the centre of the cake comes out clean. Remove from the oven.
5. Cool the cake in the tin for about 15 minutes, then transfer from the tin on to a serving plate.
6. In a cup, combine the icing sugar with the warm milk until the mixture is smooth. Drizzle over the cake.

Calories per serving: 315
Calcium per serving: 141mg

Cottage Cheesecake

Serve with fresh strawberries or other fruit topping.

Serves 12

Crust:
125g (4½ oz) digestive biscuits
55g (2 oz) margarine, softened
2 tablespoons sugar

Filling:
900g (2 lb) low fat cottage cheese, drained
170g (6 oz) sugar
3 eggs, lightly beaten
1 teaspoon vanilla essence

Topping:
240ml (8 fl oz) natural yogurt, drained of
   excess liquid (If a firm topping is desired,
   hang yogurt as in recipe for Yogurt
   Cheese, page 116, for 1-2 hours)
2½ tablespoons sugar
½ tablespoon vanilla essence

1. Preheat the oven to 350°F (180°C/Gas
   Mark 4).
2. Make the crust. Crush the digestive
   biscuits with a rolling pin or in a food
   processor. Turn into a bowl and mix with
   the margarine and sugar until the mixture
   resembles fine breadcrumbs. Press into
   the bottom of a 22.5cm (9-inch) cake tin
   with a removable base. Bake for 10
   minutes and remove from the oven.
3. Make the filling. Blend the cottage cheese,
   sugar, eggs and vanilla essence in a
   blender or food processor until smooth.
   Pour over the base in the prepared tin
   and bake until firm, about 40 minutes.
   Remove from the oven and cool.
4. Make the topping. Blend the yogurt,
   sugar and vanilla essence together.
   Spread over the baked cheesecake, cool
   and refrigerate for several hours or
   overnight before serving.

Calories per serving: 245
Calcium per serving: 100mg

Frozen Orange Yogurt

This is as good as soft-serve and easy to make at home.

Serves 9

1 packet orange jelly
170g (6 oz) sugar
240ml (8 fl oz) water
240ml (8 fl oz) orange juice
480ml (16 fl oz) natural yogurt
240ml (8 fl oz) evaporated whole milk,
   chilled

Also needed:
2 chilled metal bowls (small and large)
chilled whisks

1. Combine jelly, sugar and water in a saucepan. Boil, stirring constantly, until sugar and jelly are dissolved. Remove from heat and cool to room temperature, about 30 minutes.
2. When jelly mixture is cool, stir in orange juice and yogurt. Pour into a shallow tin and freeze, stirring occasionally, until partially frozen, 2-3 hours.
3. Spoon the yogurt mixture into a large chilled bowl. Beat with a chilled whisk until very smooth. In the smaller chilled bowl, whip the evaporated milk until stiff. Fold the whipped milk into the yogurt mixture. Spoon into a bowl or freezer container, cover and freeze until firm, 3-4 hours.

Calories per serving: 181
Calcium per serving: 168mg

Peach Ice Lollies

A light summery treat that is good any time of the year.

Serves 12

1 lb peaches sliced, peeled and puréed or a
  14 oz (395 g) tin (if unsweetened peaches
  are used, add 4 tablespoons sugar to
  juice)
1 sachet gelatine
480ml (16 fl oz) natural yogurt

Also needed:
12 x 90ml (3 fl oz) paper cups
12 wooden ice lolly sticks (or ice lolly
  moulds)

1. Thaw peaches completely. Press
   thoroughly to remove all juice and
   reserve.
2. Place drained juice (and sugar if used) in
   a saucepan and sprinkle with gelatine.
   Cook over a low heat, stirring until
   gelatine dissolves. Remove from the heat.
3. Blend peaches, yogurt and gelatine
   mixture in a blender until smooth. Place
   paper cups in a baking tin and fill with
   the fruit mixture. Cover each cup with
   greaseproof paper; make a slit in the
   paper over the centre of each cup and
   insert a stick for each lolly. Alternatively,
   fill ice lolly moulds. Freeze until firm.
4. Run warm water on the outside of each
   cup or mould to loosen it from the lolly
   before serving.

Calories per serving: 73
Calcium per serving: 70mg

Fruit and Spice Rice Pudding

Not too sweet, this pudding makes a nice afternoon or evening snack.

Serves 16

100g (3½ oz) skimmed milk powder
800ml (27 fl oz) skimmed milk
195g (7 oz) white rice, cooked pinch of salt
195g (7 oz) honey
2 eggs, beaten
1 teaspoon ground cinnamon
½ teaspoon ground ginger
335g (12 oz) orange segments, chopped
240ml (8 fl oz) orange or vanilla flavoured
   yogurt, to serve

1. Preheat the oven to 350°F (180°C/Gas Mark 4).
2. In a saucepan, blend skimmed milk powder with liquid milk until smooth. Add the rice and salt and heat to near boiling, stirring once or twice. Reduce the heat, cover and simmer for 14 minutes; do not stir. The rice should be tender, but the liquid will not be absorbed. Remove from the heat.
3. Stir in the honey, eggs, cinnamon and ginger. Spread one-third of the rice mixture in a greased 1.5-litre (2½ pint) casserole. Carefully spread half the oranges over the rice. Repeat layering the rice and oranges and top with the remaining rice.
4. Bake for 25 minutes. Remove from the oven and cool slightly.
5. Chill for several hours before serving. Top each serving with yogurt.

Calories per serving: 193
Calcium per serving: 150mg

Prune Whip

Serves 8

170g (6 oz) stoned chopped prunes
3 egg whites
70g (2½ oz) sugar
½ teaspoon ground cinnamon
¼ teaspoon salt
1 tablespoon lemon juice
30g (1 oz) hazelnuts, chopped

Whipped topping:
240ml (8 fl oz) evaporated skimmed milk,
    chilled
1 tablespoon lemon juice
3 tablespoons sugar
1 teaspoon vanilla essence

Also needed:
chilled metal bowl
chilled whisks

1. Preheat the oven to 350°F (180°C/Gas Mark 4).
2. Blend prunes in a food processor or blender until smooth.
3. In a mixing bowl whisk the prunes, egg whites, sugar, cinnamon and salt until stiff. Fold in the lemon juice and hazelnuts. Pour into an ungreased 1.5-litre (2½-pint) casserole.
4. Place the casserole in a baking tin in the oven. Pour very hot water, 2.5cm (1 inch) deep into the baking tin. Bake, uncovered until puffed and a thin film has formed on top, 30-35 minutes. Remove from the oven.
5. Make the whipped topping. Pour the evaporated milk into a chilled bowl and whip with a chilled whisk until foamy. Add the lemon juice and whip until stiff. (Whipped milk will hold its shape for up to 1 hour if refrigerated.)
6. Serve warm with whipped topping.

Calories per serving: 131
Calcium per serving: 108mg

Pumpkin Custard

Serves 6

85g (3 oz) skimmed milk powder
360ml (12 fl oz) evaporated skimmed milk
3 eggs, slightly beaten
110g (4 oz) soft dark brown sugar
450g (1 lb) pumpkin purée (see page 126)
1 teaspoon salt
1 teaspoon ground cinnamon
$\frac{1}{2}$ teaspoon ground ginger
$\frac{1}{2}$ teaspoon ground cloves
freshly grated nutmeg

1. Preheat oven to 350°F (180°C/Gas Mark 4).
2. In a bowl, blend the skimmed milk powder with the evaporated milk. In another bowl, mix together the eggs, sugar, pumpkin purée, salt, cinnamon, ginger and cloves. Stir in the milk gradually.
3. Pour into 6 ovenproof custard cups; grate nutmeg over.
4. Place the custard cups in a baking tin in the oven. Pour very hot water into the tin to within 1.25cm ($\frac{1}{2}$ inch) of the top of the cups. Bake until a knife inserted halfway between the centre and the edge comes out clean, about 45 minutes. Remove from the oven.
5. Serve either warm or chilled.

Calories per serving: 205
Calcium per serving: 304mg

Special Baked Apple

Serves 2

1 large baking apple
$\frac{1}{4}$ teaspoon ground cinnamon
1 tablespoon firmly packed dark brown
  sugar
240ml (8 fl oz) natural yogurt

1. Preheat oven to 375°F (190°C/Gas Mark 5).
2. Core and slice the apple and arrange in a small baking dish. Top with cinnamon and sugar and bake, uncovered until tender, about 40 minutes, stirring the apple slices after 20 minutes. Remove from the oven.
3. Divide the apple slices between 2 serving dishes and top with the yogurt.

Calories per serving: 164
Calcium per serving: 222mg

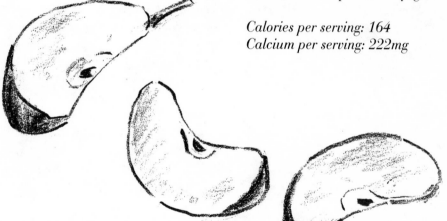

APPENDIX: FOOD SOURCES OF CALCIUM

SOURCE	CALCIUM (mg)	CALORIES
Dairy		
Cheese, 30g (1 oz)		
Blue	162	100
Cheddar	224	114
Edam	207	85
Emmenthal	272	107
Feta	140	75
Gouda	205	85
Gruyère	287	125
Mozzarella	183	72
Parmesan	342	115
Provolone	214	100
Stilton	100	130
Cheese, processed cheddar, low fat (1 slice)	134	34
Cheese, ricotta, 110g (4 oz)	257	216
Cheese, cottage, low fat, 110g (4 oz)	66	66
Cocoa powder, 1 tbsp	20	47
Ice cream, vanilla, 133g (5 oz)	196	234
Milk		
evaporated, skimmed,120ml (4 fl oz)	368	87
evaporated, whole,120ml (4 fl oz)	314	177
semi-skimmed, 240ml (8 fl oz)	269	131
skimmed, 240ml (8 fl oz)	291	74
skimmed milk powder, 50g (scant 2 oz)	595	177
whole, 240ml (8 fl oz)	269	146

SOURCE	CALCIUM (mg)	CALORIES
Milk shake, vanilla, 280ml (10 fl oz)	329	352
Whipped evaporated whole milk, 2 tablespoons	27	14
Yogurt, low fat, vanilla, 240ml (8 fl oz)	380	181
Yogurt, low fat, fruit, 240ml (8 fl oz)	358	213
Yogurt, low fat, natural, 240ml (8 fl oz)	403	116

Proteins

SOURCE	CALCIUM (mg)	CALORIES
Almonds, 30g (1 oz)	83	221
Anchovies, tinned, 8 fillets	47	49
Brazil nuts, 30g (1 oz)	65	226
Clams, fresh, 100g ($3\frac{1}{2}$ oz), 5 large	69	80
Clams, tinned, 85g (3 oz)	55	52
Egg, scrambled with milk, 1 large	47	85
Hazelnuts, 30g (1 oz)	71	181
Herring, raw 100g ($3\frac{1}{2}$ oz) (including boxes)	33	234
Lobster, raw, 100g ($3\frac{1}{2}$ oz)	62	119
Mackerel, raw, 100g ($3\frac{1}{2}$ oz) (including boxes)	24	223
Mussels, raw, 100g ($3\frac{1}{2}$ oz)	88	66
Oysters, raw, 5-8 medium-size	94	66
Pulses, 100g ($3\frac{1}{2}$ oz) dried, cooked		
Chick peas	64	144
Haricot beans	65	93
Kidney beans, Broad beans	65	93
Soya beans	21	48
Salmon, tinned , 100g ($3\frac{1}{2}$ oz)	93	155
Sardines, tinned (in oil), 100g ($3\frac{1}{2}$ oz), 8 medium	460	334
Scallops, 100g ($3\frac{1}{2}$ oz)	120	105
Sesame seeds, 30g (1 oz)	35	167
Shrimp, tinned, 100g ($3\frac{1}{2}$ oz)	110	94
Sole, raw, 100g ($3\frac{1}{2}$ oz)	17	81
Sunflower seeds, 30g (1 oz)	44	203
Tofu, firm, processed with calcium sulphate, 85g (3 oz)	861	183
Tofu, regular, processed with added calcium, 85g (3 oz)	434	94

SOURCE	CALCIUM (mg)	CALORIES
without added calcium, 85g (3 oz)	130	94

Vegetables

SOURCE	CALCIUM (mg)	CALORIES
Artichoke, globe, 1 large	51	44
Broccoli, fresh, cooked, 1 large stalk	76	18
Broccoli, frozen, cooked, 110g (4 oz)	37	27
Broccoli, raw, 1 stalk	100	25
Cabbage, cooked, 70g (2½ oz)	37	17
Endive, raw, 10 long leaves	41	10
Fennel, raw, 170g (6 oz)	67	19
Greens, cooked, 70g (2½ oz)		
Kale	89	19
Spinach (3½ oz)	600	30
Swiss chard	61	15
Spring greens (3½ oz)	86	10
Lettuce, cos, 55g (2 oz)	51	14
Okra, frozen, cooked, 85g (3 oz)	72	26
Pak choi (mustard cabbage), cooked, 85g (3 oz)	126	12
Parsley, chopped, 2 tablespoons	50	3
Swede, diced, cooked, 85g (3 oz)	42	18
Sweet Potato, baked, 1 large (3½ oz)	21	85
Watercress, raw, 10 sprigs	15	2

Fruits

SOURCE	CALCIUM (mg)	CALORIES
Blackberries, raw, 140g (5 oz)	88	41
Currants, dried, 85g (3 oz)	62	204
Figs, dried, 5	280	213
Orange, navel, 1 medium	56	65
Papaya, 1 medium	72	117
Prunes, 10	43	201

Grains

SOURCE	CALCIUM (mg)	CALORIES
Bread, white, 1 slice (av)	20	50
Bread, wholemeal, 1 slice (av)	5	43

SOURCE	CALCIUM (mg)	CALORIES
Roll, brown or white (av)	60	150
Scone, 5cm (2-inch) diameter	200	124
Taco, corn, 15cm (6-inch) diameter	60	67
Drop scones	40	95
Miscellaneous		
Beans, baked in tomato sauce, tinned, 110g (4 oz)	50	72
Custard, baked, 110g (4 oz) cup	146	132
Treacle, 1 tablespoon	75	39
Pizza, cheese, ¼ of 30cm, (12-inch) pie	291	326
Soup		
Cream of chicken, tinned,		
made with milk, 240ml (8 fl oz)	180	191
Cream of mushroom, tinned,		
made with milk, 240ml (8 fl oz)	178	203

The above figures are from McCance & Widdowson *The Composition of Foods*, HMSO, where available; otherwise manufacturers' or American data used.

INDEX